Create Together

Our Voices, Our hands,
Our Lives.

Create Together

Selection and introduction by
Sonia Thompson and Sandra Pollock OBE

First published in 2021 by SanRoo Publishing in Leicestershire,
UK.

Cover image by Sandra Pollock
Cover designed by Jerusha Barnett-Cameron

Proudly published by SanRoo Publishing in March 2021,
26 Bramble Way, Leicester, LE3 2GY, Leicestershire, UK.
www.sanroopublishing.co.uk

ISBN 978-1-8384077-0-4

Contents

Introduction

The past twelve months has been a year like no other. Covid has devastated communities, families have lost loved ones and many workers have been furloughed or lost their jobs. Leicester has felt the brunt of this pandemic, having the great misfortune of being the most locked down city in the entire UK. When Sandra and I thought about these issues, we wondered what we might do to best meet the wellbeing needs of some of the most vulnerable to the impact of Covid i.e. ethnic minority women living within the area.

Why this group you might ask? The government's own statistics have shown that African-Caribbean and Asian people are more likely to be infected by Covid. They are also more likely to die than the general population. Women's employment have also been more impacted by Covid than men's. They are more likely to be home schooling their children, and are traditionally responsible for looking after the family's health. If anyone would be in need of wellbeing support during this pandemic, it was going to be the ethnic minority women of Leicester.

The 'Create Together' project is Inspiring You's response to that need. Based on the government's 'Five Ways to Wellbeing', beneficiaries were given the opportunity to look after their physical and mental wellbeing through exercise, arts and crafts, self-confidence and creative writing sessions. We designed these spaces for like-minded women to encourage social networks and reduce loneliness. It was a place where beneficiaries could look after and support one another, and create a community of their own.

The results of the project have been astounding. We have

learned and grown with each other, and have moved forward to become much stronger in many different ways.

In this anthology we offer to all those involved and beyond, a glimpse into our journey through the art and the words of the women of the 'Create Together' project.

Enjoy!

Sonia Thompson and Sandra Pollock OBE

We are delighted to note that funding from the Coronavirus Community Support Fund, distributed by The National Lottery Community Fund, made it possible for us to create and provide the Create Together programme.

In partnership with

HM Government

THE NATIONAL LOTTERY COMMUNITY FUND

Testimonials from some of the programme participants

"I feel really lucky to have stumbled across these workshops. Having done other creative writing courses previously, I've actually learnt the most doing these workshops and felt at ease during the sessions. It's been an amazing uplifting experience that I know will continue to impact on what I write, do and say."

- Susan Doram

"Cannot believe how fast the last six months of this pandemic have flown by whilst participating in the 'Create Together' programme. Through physical exercises, Arts and Crafts and Creative Writing sessions, the programme has inspired me to find ways of maintaining my physical and mental agility, whilst having fun and making friends with amazing people of different backgrounds.

"The Creative Writing sessions, in particular, have provided a forum to develop closer friendships, and share hopes, anxieties and fears with like-minded people. Through gentle coaxing, and introducing me to different writing-styles, the sessions have encouraged me to put my pen in motion, be true to myself and be proud to share my inner feelings and experiences. This process has helped me to grow.

"Sandra and Sonya both are meticulous and passionate in the work they do and have shared their talents generously in a very caring way. Thank you very much and I recommend any sessions with them."

- Hansa Jethwa

Made by Susan Doram

Reflection

by Susan Doram

Staring in the mirror he looks at his reflection
Cold air from an open window makes him brace.
He sees and finally admires all of his imperfections.

Counselling and pills are helping with the depression.
For so long he'd been lost in such a dark, dark space.
Staring in the mirror he looks at his reflection.

His hands move over his chest as he does his daily inspection.
They slowly glide over a nipple that is out of place.
He sees and finally admires all of his imperfections.

Months of chemo, radiotherapy and operations.
Have left an angry white scar that is easy to trace.
Staring in the mirror he looks at his reflection.

His life has been given an added extension.
An opportunity that he is not going to waste.
He sees and finally admires all of his imperfections.

He smiles, his dimples leave a lasting impression.
As the morning sunlight shines brightly on his face.
Staring in the mirror he looks at his reflection.
He sees and finally admires all of his imperfections.

Simaima

by Susan Doram

Black and beautiful.
Her looks are undisputable.

Always admired with total adoration.
The catalyst for my many conversations.

You can't believe the joy that she brings.
Helping me through so many things.

A constant through the unfamiliarity.
The true reason behind my popularity.

We've been to so many places together.
And battled through some terrible painful weather.

A millstone around my neck at times.
Especially when we're tackling those hard climbs.

Sometimes she can be a pain in the backside.
But she can also be freeing which is an upside.

Let me introduce you to Simaima.
An Anglophone would call her Jemima.

She's my amazingly beautiful, black bike.
Who I guess I really, really like.

An Early Start

by Susan Doram

My face scrunched up as I sniffed the air. It smelt of stale cigarettes. I was stood in the middle of a furnished common-area, in a hotel I shared with another guest. On the floor, next to my feet were my packed bags. There was an overflowing ash tray on a table. I picked it up and flung the contents into a blue denim baseball cap, spun the hat around, then chucked the remains back into the ashtray.

The cap belonged to a French guy in the adjacent room. Last night, his very loud, drunken phone conversation in the common-room had kept me awake until 3 am. He'd disregarded my numerous polite requests to quietly continue his conversation in his room. My head started to throb from tiredness and outrage that he had felt so entitled, and how, at the time, I had felt so powerless.

My eyes narrowed as I continued to scan the room, looking for some way that I could get some vengeance. It was difficult to think of something that would be on a par with him depriving me of my sleep.

Picking up my bags to leave, I walked past his room. The door was wide open. My nose crinkled. He was sprawled across his bed in his bright orange underpants, fast asleep. The key to his room was in the door.

"I could always lock him in his room. But he was an unreasonable bastard last night; he could be an arsehole all the time. He could damage the door and ruin the hotel's property trying to get out of his room," I deliberated.

Padding across the room to the exit, I turned around and cast an eye over the room one last time, desperately trying to find that one thing that could be done to get my own back, but nothing jumped out at me. I shrugged, left the room and went to my bicycle, *Simaima*.

She was parked in the hotel owner's kitchen next to the French chap's motorbike. I put my hand in my pocket and felt for my Swiss army knife, and spun it around in my hand. Crouching down in between his motorbike and my cycle, and slowly loading her up with my bags, I glanced at the motorbike tyres, then darted my eyes over to the closed kitchen door. I slowed my breath and listened closely for footsteps.

"Could I stab a hole into his tyre before anyone sees me," I started to consider, continuing to rotate my knife in my pocket. "But, if I get caught in the act that could seriously bugger things up."

I strapped my last bag to my bicycle and put my penknife away. As I was about to leave, the hotel owner entered the kitchen. He dashed in front of me, held the front door open and waved me goodbye. I threw my leg over my bicycle and started to pedal.

"If you hadn't had dithered so much and slashed the tyre as soon as you got into the kitchen you would have got away with it," I chided myself. "Yeah, but the owner might have noticed the flat or my knife could have got stuck in the tyre."

These thoughts bounced back and forth in my head as I cycled off in search for breakfast.

I found a small restaurant run by a little old lady. Parking up my bicycle, I gave my usual smile, pointed at the food and mimed that I wanted something to eat.

I didn't have a clue as to what it was, but there were quite a few older customers sat there eating, so I figured that it must be good. She started talking to me. I tilted my head towards her whilst listening to the rhythm of her speech and the way that she pronounced her words as she ushered me to a seat. I smiled at her and tried to imagine what it was that she was saying to me.

She brought me over a bowl of soup, a coffee and a pot of jasmine tea. I'd learnt during my month here that the tea is drunk as a refreshing chaser to the coffee. I had loved the food, especially the traditional breakfast of rice and pork which set me up for the day, but this soup wasn't exactly what I had expected. It was salty, meaty, extremely chewy and muddy brown in colour. Scrutinising it further, there was something in there that looked like white meat. I took another mouthful; my second taste confirmed what I had initially suspected; I was munching on innards. I chuckled. Fortunately, I'm not a fussy eater, and if the locals are eating it then it's not going to kill me. I continued to chomp my way through the soup, polished off my drinks and got on the road.

Chelsea Rodgers by Prince blasted out of my blue tooth speaker as I drifted along the smooth tarmac. My grip on the handlebars momentarily tightened as my mind flitted back to the cigarette ash. The rhythmic movement of my legs brought me back to today's adventure, my grip loosened and the corners of my mouth started to lift.

The morning sun was bright, the sky was blue and clear and the temperature was just right, and not yet the usual hot and humid I had grown to expect of South East Asia. Today, I was heading west, leaving Vietnam and looking forward to discovering Cambodia.

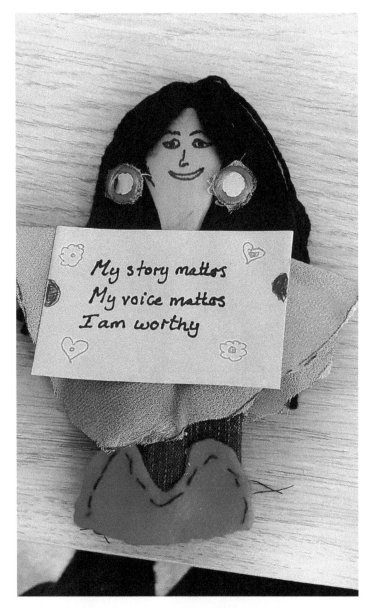

Made by Dipika Hindocha

Did the pandemic make you prisoner?
by Dipika Hindocha

Did the pandemic make you prisoner?
Did Lockdown empower your inhibitor?
Did 2020 make you feel like you were going under?
Or did it only highlight that your mind had imprisoned you…
as others were

Christian, Sikh, Hindu or Islamic
Are we all equal in the storm of the pandemic?
Where did you go in your mind to escape, when you realised
your thoughts were endemic
Did 2020 bring you opportunity to choose?
Or did you anger, rage, hate and blame… until it was bubonic

Did the pandemic really make you prisoner?
In your mind, did you bring up every misnomer?
Did 2020 give you time to reflect?
Or did you stew in anger, rage, hate and blame… and refuse
to become a listener

Did the pandemic do you a favour?
Or did it embolden your jailor
Did 2020 make you feel a failure?
Or did your mind stay measured… and change your behaviour

Did the pandemic slow your progress?
Or did your mind use every power to build a fortress
Did 2020 make you weave a tapestry of despair in your brain,
like a seamstress

Where in your mind did you go for hope?
When unpicking the weave only led to more fatigue and stress

Who will you be my dear, when you finally manage to release this?
Will your mind finally feel bliss?
Or will 2020 forever keep you in the abyss
Did the pandemic make you realise there was something amiss?
Or did your heart always whisper 'you can my dear, liberate this'.

Fear not my child, for I am at peace

by Dipika Hindocha

On the twenty third of March twenty twenty-one,
One year since the first lockdown begun,

A day of reflection has been announced,
To remember those who left and were pronounced,
Who could not see this day -
The twenty third of March twenty twenty-one.

To those who had to say goodbye from an LCD screen,
And not get to hold their loved ones' hand,
Or give them a hug, like they had planned.

For those who want to believe, fear not,
Their soul knows you cared,
Their soul wants peace,
They know you were scared.

What lessons have we learned
About life and death,
Those of us who still have breath?

For sure, we must respect and remember,
Those who did not make it to twenty twenty-one,
But what would they say?

From their new place of rest,
If they could send you a message,
What would they suggest?

Would they want you to feel guilt, pain and remorse?
Or live life to the full,
With even greater might and force?

Perhaps they might say, "Fear not my child,
For I am at peace.
Go forth and live
To the fullest you can.

"Give your best in the life you have,
Live not with regret for the words unspoken,
Give your all to those with you still,
Give them life; through your gifts of love, let them fill.

"And fear not my child, for I am at peace,
At peace with you,
With me,
And with the world.

"Fear not my child, I felt your love.
Through the LCD screen,
Your message reached me,
As though from a white dove."

Every Guest is God
by Dipika Hindocha

"Woohoo...Hello Mukta…"

"I've come te huv a wee cuppa coffee wi ye so y dunny get lonely, Mukta."

It's Mrs Panzeeca from the downstairs flat. Everyone calls her Panzeeca. She carries an air of authority with the residents of the two storey flats we live in. A heavy smoker, tall, slim, dark hair. Streetwise, brisk, straight talking, no nonsense but strangely exuding a sophisticated Italian-like quality.

"Oh yes! yes!" My mother nods and smiles politely.

Her eyes light up as she welcomes the company, even though she cannot speak much English.

Her four-foot nine body shuffles along the hallway, her old, faded brown and yellow sari sweeping the floor as she goes. She appears to glide, like a dalek.

Her size-three feet are barely visible under her sari, holding up the weight of her over inflated-stomach (which I later find out is a remnant of many miscarriages and below-par medical treatments in Uganda).

Her well-oiled hair is sleekly pinned to her head, plaited neatly, trailing off to the finest tip, ending right on her bum. I used to wonder how she managed to avoid sitting on it when she went to the loo! How fiddly must it have been, lifting a sari up with its five-point-five metres of printed polyester and making sure your plaited hair didn't get caught between your bum and the toilet seat.

But it's not the sort of question a good, dutiful Gujarati girl was supposed to ask.

The beaming smile on Ba's face and excitement of

receiving a friendly visitor; she loved the company of our
Scottish neighbours. Welcoming them with offers of bhajia,
gathia, rotli, shak, poori, thepla whatever they wanted was no
trouble.

Koi pan apda ghare awe ene bhagwan ni jem jamarwana.

(Whoever comes to our house should be fed as though you
were feeding God himself.)

And in return, they would sit and patiently teach her
English, reading Janet and John books, the same ones I
was being given at the new primary school I walked myself
to every morning. I remember feeling proud of her but
embarrassed all at the same time.

Ba's wheezy chest hisses with constriction, asthma
restricting her ability to stand, walk or just expend energy.
Everything she does is in slow motion to preserve her breaths.

She ushers Panzeeca into our kitchen; stained orange
cupboards with formica worktops and 'harvest gold' coloured
walls in need of attention.

"Come come, I make you cuppa masala tea."

'Oooccch nooo Mukta, I canny drink tea wi spices innit!
Thats just no right!'

My heart pounds...

'Please, please Ba don't offer her stuff with smelly spices
in it! Kids at school will find out... and they'll tell me I
smell.'

'Och a wee cuppe coffee'll de me nicely.'

'You like some gathia? Me made...myself,' Ba says in her
pigeon English, nodding as though urging Panzeeca to
eat...she has to eat something.

Guests are Gods you know! It's bad luck if they leave
without having had something to eat. And you are not a good,
selfless Hindu if you do not go out of your way to offer your

guest - I mean God - some food and a warm welcome.

This hospitality was to be extended to anyone we met; teachers, shopkeepers and neighbours alike. Don't rock the boat, be grateful, be humble, be giving, show respect.

But outside of the house my experience could be treacherous. The sons of other neighbours we were to 'respect' called me 'Da-Pee-Ka Da-Paki' and told me I smelt of curry.

I'd say nothing, keep my head down. Suppressing the rumblings of anger and fear bubbling up in my heart, pushing my feelings down into my stomach. Internal strength from watching my parents' resolve. Resilience being built, to survive the hard knocks life would throw at me again and again.

Ba and Panzeeca exchange faltered conversations at the kitchen table; Panzeeca giving much needed advice to Ba on the ins and outs of living and surviving in the new territory we tried to grapple with.

Bapuji is in the living room, watching the news for updates on politics. The black and white television encased in orange plastic, running on metered fifty-pence coins. The screen shows reruns and commentary of the 'Rivers of Blood' speech by Enoch Powell, given a few years earlier in 1968.

'Kone khabar che apadne a UK ma ketli var revadese aloko.' (Who knows how long we will be allowed to stay in this country.)

The duality of our existence has continued. Confusion; trust and safety questioned daily.

We were also guests, were we not - in this country?

And so began my juxtaposed life, between two cultures. Never quite fitting in. Too Indian to be White, too White to be Indian.

Made by Rohita Chauhan

Despair And Hope

by Mala Kotechas

She was walking in the beautiful sunshine.
All of a sudden it turned dark.
What happened?
She went shopping and got scared to see all the people
wearing masks.
What happened?
She had a lot of friends, yet she felt isolated.
What happened?
She could not sleep, and the nights were as long as the days.
What happened?
Days were turning into weeks, and weeks into months.
Time seemed to be dragging yet the year had nearly ended.
What happened?
She was watching her grandchildren on facetime,
And missing out on seeing them grow up. Would they
remember her?
What happened?
Diwali came and went; Christmas came and went.
She was losing herself.
What happened?
In the new year, she realised her life had changed forever.
What happened?
Today on the news, she heard the government saying that
things were going to get better.
What was happening?
The next morning, she woke up to hazy sunshine and found
herself smiling.
It was as if she had woken up from a bad dream.

She knew it would be a different world.
The sun was trying break through the clouds.
Hope happened!

I Am Lucky To Be Alive

by Mala Kotecha

Our world is a beautiful place.
The mountains, the lakes, the rivers & the oceans.
I am lucky to be alive.
And to be amongst nature,
Why had I forgotten that?

Our world is a beautiful place.
To be able to wake up every day,
To see the sunshine and hear the birds sing.
I am lucky to be alive.

Looking out of the window, watching the squirrels leaping
from branch to branch.
The cat sitting there, amused.

Our world is a beautiful place.
Going for a walk in the park,
Hearing the children giggling and playing.
I am lucky to be alive.

Even though surrounded by sadness and the shadows of death,
Appreciating the nature we have so neglected.
Our world is a beautiful place.
I am lucky to be alive.

Short Poem Collection
by Mala Kotecha

Faith, Love, Hope

Have faith, love and hope,
Riding my spirits to great heights.
Stay there, please stay there.

Everyday

Night and day, everyday,
Wait for you both with enthusiasm,
Come sunshine, come moonlight.

LOVE

Dare to Love again,
Even though your heart's been betrayed,
Wait for true love to happen.

The sound of silence

What was the noise I was hearing?
It was a very quiet night.
The trees and plants were still.
The whole world seemed to be asleep.
Yet I felt so restless.
Then I realized, it was the sound of my heartbeats.

Heart Break

by Mala Kotecha

Jane stopped in her tracks. The loud explosion froze her feet. Across the road, a warehouse set further back had a lot of smoke coming out. People were moving away from that side of the street.

And then she saw him. Him, who had been part of her life for three years, whose death had left a big void in her life, mind and heart.

He was striding away with the same hurried walk. The same style of dress and the same tousled hair.

Surely that was not possible. She could feel her legs giving way and tried to steady herself. She could hear the sirens of police cars, ambulances and fire brigades.

A policeman walked up to her and asked her to move.

She said to him, "My husband's there."

He looked confused. "No, Mam. That is a derelict empty building."

He could see the panic on her face and asked her to sit in the police car whilst he made some inquiries.

He came back with his colleague and asked her when she had last seen him. When she said two years ago, he looked a bit annoyed but the look disappeared as quickly as it came.

"Is there anyone I can call for you?"

She nodded and gave him her friend, Jill's number. He spoke with Jill, then passed the phone over to her. Jill sounded very worried and asked if she was okay.

She started telling her, but she said, "Jane, I am really sorry, I am in a meeting. As soon as its finished I will drive down to wherever you are."

At first she felt let down. Then she remembered Jill was one person who was always there for her and couldn't always drop everything and come down.

She thanked the policemen and left them her details in case they had any news. As she was walking away, she couldn't help but wonder what they were thinking.

The sun was beating down and she walked through the park with tears streaming down her face. She found an empty bench in her favourite spot. There was a young mum playing with her two children, who were giggling and running around.

She sat there for what seemed like ages, with a million thoughts going through her mind. They had never recovered his body. He and his friends were on a day out, mountain-climbing, and he had met with an accident. Apparently they had tried hard to find him, but in vain.

Was their married life just a lie? They seemed happy, but was it just a façade? Her mind was all muddled up. Yet she knew that she had just seen him.

Then a penny dropped. He was a coward, and rather than facing her he had decided to stage this. Or was her imagination running away again?

All of a sudden she felt like she had woke up from a bad dream. A dream where she had lost the best part of five years of her life.

'At the end of the day,' she thought, 'We are each responsible for our own life and happiness. If we hold anyone else accountable then we are wasting our time. And now enough of grief, guilt, sadness and loneliness.'

Should she try and find him? Maybe someday she would know the truth or maybe never, but she was not going to waste anymore of her life.

Her phone rang. It was Jill. She sounded really stressed. "Are you okay Jane? I have been trying to reach you for the past hour."

She replied, "Jill can I buy you dinner?"

Jill sounded really surprised. "Has something happened?"

Jane replied, "It's like I have been reborn and its my birthday today. Can you pick me up at seven?"

Jill sounded relieved. "I can't wait."

Painting by Surbhi Rayarel

Journey through dusk and dawn

by Surbhi Rayarel

What a dark scary night it seems, this journey with Covid.
It's horrid.
Listening to the news of losses and trauma, people are facing.
My heart is racing.

They are tracing the virus.
There is silence everywhere.
The roads are empty or deserted.
The drastic fall in the number of shoppers in the shopping malls.
The time, seems stopping, not hopping.
What a scary night! It seems, this journey with Covid.
It's horrid.

Missing the vital contact with friends.
Children and grandchildren, I crave for your hugs and kisses.
Missing all the hustle and bustle with the gatherings of friends and family,
Exchanging news and views, seems like an unreachable dream.
The Covid has eclipsed all the human contacts.
What a dark scary night, it seems
It's horrid.

Oh! The vaccination bringing rays of hope.
Like a fairy with her magic wand.
Vision of new hope, new dreams and new world are the survival rope.

New journey with more insight into humanity, appreciation and consideration of nature that's what we, the earth creatures crave for.
What a dark and scary night it seems, this journey with Covid.

To free us from this Covid fright
Just waiting for the dawn to bring the bright light

Sleep

By Surbhi Rayarel

Can hear the bleep in the distance.
The buzzing of the bees.
The singing of the birds.
The soothing hum of a spinning washing machine.
The howling of the wind,
above the TV's high pitched voices from the people chatting.

I put the duvet cover halfway over my face and close my eyes.
So many thoughts, memories starts flashing in my head.
Sleep performs a vanishing act.
I open my eyes.
In the pitch darkness, I visualise the day's hustle and bustle.

Again I close my eyes in an attempt to sleep.
Turning and tossing for - God knows - several hours.
At last, sleep bestows its magic on me.

Deep in slumber, I hear someone talking:
'Get up now, Usha, it's mid-day!'
Try to open my eyes but no joy.
I turn and go back to sleep.
My much awaited sleep.

Us

By Surbhi Rayarel

A platform of voices,
Providing choices,
To express, to explore and reflect
And put our pen in motion,
An awesome opportunity to discard fears
And share our emotions,
To proceed in life's journey
With hope, dreams and determination.
The programme has provided an excellent opportunity
For unlocking potential in lockdown
I would greatly recommend it to others.

Saffron from Spain

by Surbhi Rayarel

"What a relief! We have been worried about you, Sweta,"
exclaimed Rajiv.

He often called me Sweta, when he wasn't calling me
Mum. It was a hangover from when we worked together
as colleagues. He took my hand and reassuringly led me
towards the plane waiting for us. Before that, he thanked the
gentleman who brought me over. Happiness shone on my
face; I walked towards the plane, feeling safe and secure.

I said to Rajiv, "Thank you very much, I have been feeling
very confused and shaken up."

In response to that he said, "Don't worry, Mum, we are
here now," and he nudged me towards the plane.

As I sat in my seat on the plane and held onto his
arm, I felt light, as if a big burden of worry were lifted
off my shoulders. A muffled announcement came over the
loudspeaker and we moved our heads to watch the activity at
the front of the plane.

"Now we request your full attention as the flight
attendants demonstrate the safety features of this aircraft.
When the seat belt sign illuminates, you must fasten your
seat belt. Insert the metal fittings one-into-another, and
tighten by pulling on the loose end of the strap."

The air hostess helped me to sit comfortably and tied my
seat belt, and the plane was soon taking off.

Everyone seemed relaxed, some sitting reading, some
looking out of the windows, resting, and some settling their
kids. All this had a calming effect on me and in no time, we

were on our way home.

As we journeyed, my mind wondered back to the Spanish departure lounge, where I had become so lost.

"Foreign land, foreign language, foreign currency, foreign people," I recalled, with a sigh.

My family was lost amidst them. They were all dispersed in the duty-free shops at the vast airport. Initially, my husband, my daughter's in-laws and I were together in a shop, looking for different items and searching for them to take back home to give as gifts. Saffron was at the top of my agenda as an item to buy, but laughter soon changed to fear, when I turned my head, and noticed that none of my family were in the vicinity. Anxiety started to creep up within me.

The question in my mind was, "Where are they? Where is Aalok?"

I started pacing from one end to another. I felt and looked lost.

"Where have they gone? Why have they deserted me?"

The questions started flooding in my head. My face covered with worry; my pace was hesitant. My heart started beating fast.

The voice in my head questioned me. "Sweta, what will you do now?

"I will call them now with my phone," thought I.

Suddenly, it dawned that I did not have my phone with me. Because of my ill health and dementia, I did not carry my purse. It was in my husband's backpack!

Although there was hustle and bustle, I was oblivious of the joy, excitement, and cheerfulness. I was lost in a maze of haze.

"Where am I going to get help from?"

My head was spinning; I was drowning in my fear and sorrow. I was amongst strangers. My mind went blank and it seemed like my heart would stop!

"Where is my family?"

I could feel beads of sweat on my forehead. I was seized with fear. I couldn't fathom it.

"Am I imagining this? Let me go to the store where we were together. Oh, shit, my memory is playing up. Do I turn left or right? I can't recall the store's name either."

Announcements were made in different languages. Confusion spread on my face. My body language, and facial expression were causing people to look at me. I was definitely not in my comfort zone.

"Who do I ring? Who do I speak with?"

Again, my mind went blank! My body felt like ice, my feet like they'd become pokers. My stomach churned. I felt tense and unsure, like I was losing control. I was full of fear, drifting in a storm.

Suddenly, a ray of hope emerged. A lady was sitting on one of the tables, having food and drinks. The lady seemed approachable. I tried and asked her.

"Will you please tell me where the airport lounge is? Our plane would soon be flying off."

She did not understand what I was saying, but pointed towards her husband, who was coming with some drinks and water in a tray. When he came towards us, she spoke to him in what sounded like German.

Her husband asked me in English, "Are you all right? How can I help you?"

My joy was boundless. Here, I had found a messiah in response. I showed him my plane ticket and he gently took my arm with reassurance and guided me towards the lounge. My lips were dry, but the water he gave me was like a lifeline. Gratefully I took few sips and thanked him.

Once in the departure lounge, I felt safe. I hoped to find my daughter or other family members. And to my relief, I saw Rajiv coming towards me.

"But Sweta, I don't understand one thing. If you did not have your purse and the phone, how did you explain to the gentleman who helped you?"

Before I had a chance to give him my answer, my daughter, Chandni, was by my side.

I slipped back in time in that moment, remembering earlier in the day when we were getting ready to go on the plane and leave Spain. Chandni had told me where everyone was.

"Dad is there in the opposite store, with my in-laws," said Chandni, "And we are going to line up with Rajiv and the children. Look over there, there is Pooja and Jay with their children." Then she turned around and gave me my passport and the ticket from her purse and said, "Mum, hold on to this. Just in case I don't see you until we board."

So, I had been holding the passport along with the ticket all the time.

'Wow! That was lucky," exclaimed Sarah.

"Oh yes, she has always been my saviour whenever I have been in trouble." I said and smiled, lost in thoughts.

I could hear Sarah calling my name again.

"Sweta, this pudding is boiling. It is on slow heat as you asked me to put it, what do we do now?"

I returned to the present.

With a bottle of saffron from Spain in my hand, I uttered, "Sorry, Sarah, I have a quarter cup of milk here. I will put few strands of saffron, warm it for 4- 5 minutes in a microwave. Stir it vigorously until the milk changes colour to orange and then we add it in the pudding. After that we let it cook for another 10 minutes or until it thickens. We shall add sugar, pistachio and almond flakes. When the sugar has melted, switch off the cooker."

Made by Hansa Jetwa

Lockdown

by Hansa Jethwa

A word that had a meaning of its own,
But is also a word that has taken its own meaning.
I am in lockdown,
She down the road is in lockdown.
No visits,
No long chats on the doorsteps,
Lest the virus jumps,
Through air,
Through the breath.
They talk about lockdown,
They tell me,
'Stay indoors,'
'Talk to others as if they have the virus,'
'Be cautious,'
'Be safe,'
Lockdown what shape have thou taken?

Freedom

by Hansa Jethwa

Freedom, oh freedom I yearn thee,
What shape and form art thou?
My mind boggles,
What shape and form art thou?

My mind boggles and questions,
Freedom from what?
Freedom to do what?
Freedom from whom?

My mind boggles and introspects,
Why yearn outside for freedom?
When inner mind is shackled.

Shackled? Yes shackled,
Shackled by fear and thoughts of what others might say.

My mind boggles and restricts,
Stopping and shackling me from freedom,
Freedom, oh freedom I yearn thee.

Yes, shackled but listening to that yearning within,
Yes, yearning for that illusive freedom.
Yes, searching and gathering the speed to attain that freedom,
Freedom, oh freedom I come to attain thee.

Breaking Free
by Hansa Jethwa

Freedom, oh freedom, I strive to attain thee,
Born as a girl in the Indian society,
Prisoned and shackled in culture, to shape my destiny.
'You are second class,' they teach and socialise me,
Born to serve men- fathers, brothers, husbands -
the list goes on.

Freedom, oh freedom how I strive to attain thee,
'Don't dress too short, or stay out too late,' as there are
consequences,
My guilt provoked and movements stifled, lest I tempt the
better half.
Prisoned and shackled in culture, to shape my destiny.
'Think not beyond cooking, cleaning and raising children,
And if bored, give a try to careers that are
natural to your kind.'

Freedom, oh freedom, I strive to attain thee,
'Think not of becoming an engineer or builder, or voting,
They are too logical and strenuous for frailty like you,'
They insist it is God's and the nature's way too.
Prisoned and shackled in culture, to shape my destiny.
I wake up with confidence and a great resolve,
To evaluate and rekindle the spirit within me.

Freedom, oh freedom, I strive and attain thee,
No longer prisoned and shackled in culture, to shape my
destiny.

Short Poems
by Hansa Jethwa

1.

Time flies,
Attending to this and that,
Not a minute to breath.

2.

Life is for living,
Enjoy the moments while you can.
Gone in a flash.

3.

Travelling in a ship,
No idea who the captain is,
Dreaming of destination afar.

Kindness

by Hansa Jethwa

What is kindness?
Giving is kindness,
Accepting is kindness,
Receiving is kindness.
In the land of harsh realities,
It only takes
A single word of kindness,
A tender, loving hand of kindness,
To change a world of one,
Bring light in the darkness,
Conquer the space between life and death.

*(Written after hearing about a young person that had
committed suicide.)*

The Night Out

by Hansa Jethwa

Gauri was going out. She was going to the cinema for the first time ever, without her parents by her side, or even them having to say whether the film was appropriate for her or not. The environment that she was growing up in was very sheltered and restricted. What society said not only mattered but played an important part; especially if you were a girl child. She was in very high spirit, humming and dancing away as she carefully chose the dress to wear.

'I better not wear too much make up, just in case some friends of my parents saw me', she thought as she applied her face cream.

She was being careful not to dress up too much, either. She continued to hum *Jindagi ek safar he suhana… …,* one of her favourite songs, as she wore her favourite turquoise dress.

'Life is one beautiful journey…'

The sentiments of the song carried on buzzing in her head as she carefully plaited her long, silky black hair.

"One day when I am old enough, I will leave my hair unplaited and loose just like the way they do in those Hindi films," she promised herself.

It was the premiere released of the film *Dr. Zivago* in the cinema. Her cousin had got tickets for her and her brothers for its first showing. On top of this, it was her first ever English film to see in a cinema. Her cousin called in. Fifteen-year-old Gauri was ready, and so were her younger two brothers. They were all thrilled and excited to go to the cinema without their parents.

Just as they were leaving their home, they heard a soft but

stern voice demanding where Gauri was going. Gauri stopped, her eyes narrowed, lips pressed and with some exasperation sighed under her breath: 'now what'. And then her eyes squinted, and lips curled as she noted that the question was directed at her only, even though her brothers were younger than she was.

She recognised the stern voice of her Dadima (paternal grandmother) and could sense her standing right behind her. She had always known her Dadima to be fair but strict, with her own ideas of rights and wrongs and things that girls, especially fifteen-year-olds, should and should not do. You see, her Dadima was born in a caste, where there were limits to the aspirations that girls could have. These were perpetuated as customs and through many rituals that were developed as part of the system. These customs were then regulated, not by the 'Law of the Land', but strangely and effectively on hearsay, and it always started with 'what will Samaj (society) say?...'.

Turning round, Gauri was face to face with this thin, tall, frail but sturdy old figure, all dressed in white, with distinct marks on the face which revealed the hardships endured over the years. Suspicions and inquisitiveness were written all over her face and on her dynamic body. Gauri's militant eyes met her Dadima's questioning eyes with a mixture of defiance. Her jaw lines were firm and there was a flash of boldness in her eyes, and then her body slumped, and eyes looked downwards to the floor, as she succumbed to the customary-learnt reverence for older people. She was fully aware that her Dadima had travelled widely the 'street' knowledge', that she had picked through these experiences, had contributed to her radiating the aura of wisdom and authority. Dadima was not shy at all about using this acquired authoritative power.

"Where are you going?" she wanted to know.

"Going to see a film," Gauri answered in a whisper, and then almost as an afterthought, she added, "With my brothers and my cousin".

"What film are you going to see?" The tone was less stern, but still inquisitive. Gauri thought the additional information had helped.

"Dr.Zivago" Gauri answered in the same quiet voice.

"What is that... er...Doctor......." Her Dadima was struggling to pronounce the foreign name.

Gauri could see that the name did not make any sense to her and was wishing that there would be no more questions. But this was not to be. Her Dadima was remarkably shrewd and continued to cross examine Gauri.

"What is the film about?"

"Ummm...errr...." Gauri faltered, and continued in a compliant quiet voice that could hardly be heard "It is an English film".

Dadima's ears pricked up, her hearing ability seem as good as that of a sixteen-year-old. "An English film?"

Gauri heard the echo of her voice only, much, much louder, with indignation and a sharp tone of disapproval. This short question from this 85-year-old, skinny but powerful lady had conveyed myriads of messages. Gauri hesitated, pretending not to understand the underlying message then blurted out.

"Mum and Dad have agreed, and I am going out with my brothers and cousin," she said with gusto but in a quiet voice, taking care not to offend or aggravate the situation in any way. She was fully aware of the consequences of making her Dadima angry or upset.

"What is happening here?" Dadima questioned in a rather loud voice and pacing the room. It was obvious that this question was aimed at Gauri's parents who were not in the room.

"The film starts in about half an hour and we have to leave now, or we will be late. We have already bought the tickets." Gauri put up all arguments all in one go as she inched towards the door with her brothers and cousin.

The skinny but agile body of her Dadima moved swiftly and barricaded the door.

"NO!" She said firmly. "The boys can go but you are not going. Your Mum and Dad have no sense, allowing a young girl like you to go see an English film. These films," she postulated, "Corrupt young minds." Before Gauri could forward any points to counteract her Dadima rebuked her with "Have you thought what the neighbours and the Samaj would say about your character and our upbringing, if they come to know that we allow you to go see an English film?"

Disenchantment and apprehension were creeping all over Gauri as she realised what the outcome of this encounter might be. Her brothers, who had until now been playing spectators role, tried to reassure their Dadima.

Her cousin - who was the oldest of them all - added "There is nothing to worry about, it is a family story, and I will look after them all".

But their Dadima was not having any of this as she continued to rationalise her decision to not allow Gauri to go to see an English film.

"Gauri is a girl, and of marriageable age. It is an age when a mind can easily be corrupted and English films are bad influences" she apportioned her profound wisdom in one breath and continued with persistence. "I was married at her age and I cannot allow any act that could prejudice Gauri's marriage chances".

It was obvious that Dadima had no experience of seeing

any English films and her arguments were based on hearsay. Besides, it seemed clear that she thought marriage was the only thing that the girls were brought in this world for. But the customs did not allow any younger ones to disregard or argue against the words of their elders, and certainly not that of their 85-year-old grandmother. Older people were revered in their culture.

Gauri's parents kept well out of the way. They knew that they did not stand any chance to voice their opinions, and feared being labelled as too liberal or told that they had lost control over their child. It dawned on Gauri that she was on her own and therefore needed to work out her own defence and arguments to change the direction of this conversation. But before she could muster any courage to whisper any words, she heard her Dadima persisting.

"What if a member of Samaj sees Gauri going to see an English film? What impression will they have of her?" The conversation had changed to a monologue, as Gauri, her brothers and her cousin all had been stunned to silence. "I cannot allow your parents to make this mistake and risk the chances of a good marriage prospect for Gauri..." She went on and on, for another minute or so outlining her rationales and concerns.

There was an element of concern in that stern old authoritative voice.

'It was not that she was a ruthless dictator', Gauri reflected in her mind with sultry look, 'but someone stuck in a time warp, stuck in the past. Yes, her Dadima had lived experiences and had gained a lot of experiences through her travels, and always thought about what was in the best interest of every member of the family', the debate in Gauri's mind continued to rage, 'but surely she could change with the times'.

Gauri made a face and was sulking as she was trying to make sense of those few minutes gone by.

'If only… if only I had decided to leave home by the back door...' Clasping her hands over her head, she thought with an air of desperation, the humming of that beautiful song had evaporated from her mind, just like that.

Gauri was heartbroken and had a sinking feeling, as she contemplated the outcome of this encounter.

Her cousin made one last futile attempt. "You know we have already bought the tickets and at this late stage we cannot sell the cinema ticket. We will have wasted our money if Gauri does not come." He hoped that the loss of money on the ticket might contribute towards altering Dadima's mind.

"Gauri is not going out," she announced commandingly taking no notice of the argument put forward. She continued in a dismissive voice "You boys better hurry along or you will all be late."

Her brothers and her cousin looked at Gauri rather apologetically as they moved towards the door and left home for the film. Gauri could sense that they all had felt that the whole episode did not make any sense and was not fair. How could what a Samaj member might say disdain one's character? And if English films were a bad influence, then where was the logic of letting the boys go? Whichever way you looked at it, Gauri knew and so did her brothers and cousin that their Dadima was the judge and the jury all wrapped up in one and her verdicts were always the final with no course for appeal.

The Advent of Corona
by Hansa Jethwa

It was the year 2019 and a big conference was to be held, attended by all living species of the world except the humans. The conference, "Reimagining Life on Planet Earth – Innovations and Inspirations" was organised to discuss the atrocities on animals, such as causing unnecessary pain and suffering in the pursuit of food, clothing, entertainment and research, by the humans. It was proposed that this species was at the height of its arrogance, plundering nature with absolutely no regard for other living creatures, polluting nature, being selfish and overusing world resources for the benefit of only themselves.

All the other forms of life were getting fed up of this human behaviour. The conference's aims were to find solutions to these human infringements. The goal: to stop them from doing further harm to Mother Earth, and to find ways of getting them to reflect on the impacts of their behaviour.

The conference had started with the review of the blue planet and its riches. Many talked about the lush green vegetation and balance of resources used and reproduced. Some films made by humans, such as Sir David Attenborough and others, were shown to highlight the amount of pollution and damage caused by humanity's disregard for its surrounding. More films highlighted atrocities to farm-animals; the extent of human greed and how some humans had to have all the resources for themselves. All of the presentations posed the same question …. 'What can be done to stop the humans from damaging the only one blue planet of the solar system?'

"What if we entered their cities and residential areas and frightened them?" said the Hyena, who always worked by creating fear in others. "The lions, tigers, elephants, snakes and many other creatures can easily carry this out," she giggled and laughed.

"It will not work," the sly Fox howled. The fox, since abandoning its diminishing natural forest habitat, has been living closely with humans in urban environments, and had varied experiences of human encounters as it made its living. He simpered as he added, "Can I remind the conference that this tactic had been tried by the tigers in India and the elephants in Africa to name a few."

"This only incited the humans to use their guns and kill them." The Camel grunted. He made awkward moves to stand up, seizing the chance to draw attention to himself and his plight in relation to camel racings.

"These humans have developed so many weapons that they can use against us," the Tiger sighed with his head bowed down in exasperation and dismay.

All at the conference thought it was rather disconcerting and painful to see such a majestic animal looking so humiliated.

"Their guns cannot harm us," the Ant said, trying to be cooperative and helpful. "We can crawl all over their cities and houses and their weapons too.... and also bite them!" she added enthusiastically.

"Come on, that is not going to work! We want them to reflect on their behaviour and become aware of the impact their behaviour is having on all of us," the Dog barked.

The humans had been good to their kind; given dogs shelter and, for most of the time, he had found them to be open to reasoning.

All the animals took notice of what the dog had to say, as they knew dogs had the closest contact with humans and as such, they could predict their responses.

The participants' bodies drooped and lips quivered, shifting their glances sideways. There was a deafening silence, as participants sought to find solutions.

After ten long minutes, the Owl, with his chin up, marched up and down the aisle, with his wings folded behind him. He broke the silence with a bold statement: "We need to think of ways which stop them from carrying out these destructive activities and give them time to reflect on the harm their actions are causing to Mother Earth."

"They are a stubborn and selfish breed and will not succumb to any reasoning," the Cat interjected, reflecting on the many battles she had had.

The time she wanted to sit high on the piano or on the top self just to keep an eye on her territory. Or when she objected to having her meal in the passageway from a deep bowl. Or even when she just used the upholstered furniture to sharpen her claws. She remembered coming to her wits end trying to get the humans to understand her point of view.

"We need to find ways to make them reflect on the impact their activities are having on other living beings on the planet," the Donkey mumbled, almost repeating the Owl's words. The Donkey was preoccupied with the thoughts of the heavy loads that he had been made to carry to and from the marketplace, at times with no food or drink.

The Owl chirped up, as he continued to march up and down and proposed, "I suggest we find ways; first to stop them from all of their daily activities, and secondly to force them to reflect on how their behaviour is unbalancing the natural world." The Owl's bold statement stirred up a commotion amongst the members.

"Stopping them from their daily activities?"

"An impossible task!"

"We cannot even get nearer to them!"

"Hmmmm……"

These and tons of other questions, comments, and murmurs were shouted, screeched, whispered amongst the contributors. The mumble of noise continued for a while and then followed another long silence. The problem in hand was especially important to all, but at the same time a difficult one to solve.

The worry on all the animals could be seen clearly. The stark reality of their natural living resources, both on the land and in the sea, either being polluted or destroyed was distressing them. The big puzzle that all the participants had was why the humans could not even comprehend that such infringements on their beloved planet could only result in the demise of all their existences. This grim reality of the possible end of Mother Earth was the force driving all that had gathered.

Suddenly, like a flash of light, the animals heard the Hen squawking, "Humans got very frightened when a virus inside me got transferred to them."

The Hyena's proposal of frightening humans had obviously left an impression on her pea head.

The Hen could sense an air of anticipation and so, enjoying the attention of all animals, continued with an air of importance. "They stopped killing us for food for a while after," she paused, flickered her eyes for a second, and carried on, "And all over the world they began to think of our welfare and how they treated us."

"Do you mean, passing a virus within you made the humans all over the world stop and think of the ways they treat you?" the Cow asked with some bewilderment, as she thought of the time when the humans fed them meat and bone meal. The Cow continued with an air of reflection. "When our kind got BSE, what they called 'Mad Cow Disease', it did not get them to think of our welfare, even when it was not us that were mad. Think what madness it is to mix meat and bone in our meal when everyone knows that we only eat grass."

There was uproar. All present were astonished, as such an action was incomprehensible.

The Cow carried on empathetically, "Instead of changing their practice, the human action was to go on a rampage to kill most of our kind, all over the world," the Cow concluded rather soberly.

"Yes, our conditions were only improved for a while," the Hen replied quietly but with insistence, as she carefully disregarded the risks that the Cow was alluding to.

"Passing a virus from inside us to humans sounds like a great proposition," the Bat woke up with excitement and fluttered around, once again completely ignoring the underlying caution from the Cow.

"Could an act like that really make the humans stop and take note of the damage they are causing to the environment?" the Owl thought aloud.

"Actually make them stop destroying the environment?" the Monkey chattered as he hopped around, his question was giving the fuel to the idea of virus transmission.

Once again, there were more questions than answers or ideas floating in the minds of all present. Frightening the humans through virus-transfer seemed to be a gamble worth taking. Glimmers of hope and a growing sense of excitement seem to grip the participants. However, there were the questions of how and what could they do, as well as which virus and from whose body.

"Whatever we do, it has to be something that is bigger and different than the virus the Hen floated, as the humans did not really take any long-term notice," the Owl interjected. "Hmmm....." there was another grim pause.

"Maybe...." the Bat said in a speculative tone, "Maybe the virus inside me could do the job. The humans have never been exposed to them, so they will have to take notice."

An air of excitement, although slightly subdued could be detected amongst the participants. No-one was sure if the virus inside the Bat could do the trick. There was also the practicality of transfer. How could this be possible? Humans did not come anywhere near the bats.

"Whatever we decide, we have to decide quickly, or Mother Earth and we all be will extinct," screeched the Rat, whose breed had made several attempts to stop humans from multiplying back in the middle ages.

"Aha!" the wise and learned Owl whispered, "There are some places in the world where bats do come into contact with humans."

Seeing wide eyes and question marks on the faces of most participants, the Bat shared, "Yes, there are some countries in the world where we and other animals such as salamanders, civets, pangolin, bamboo rats, etc. are kept alive in cages". The Bat continued with his eyes looking down and with rather sad tone. "We are then made to watch our very own brothers and sisters being slaughtered and cooked!"

All the conference members were stunned to hear this, seeing tears roll out of the Bat's eyes as he shared the information. They all felt the pain, and some who were subjected to same cruelty sympathised and nodded in acknowledgement.

Amidst the sadness, this sharing added even more resolve

for the congregants to find ways of transferring this virus to the humans, even when nobody was sure if the virus in the bat would get the humans to stop and think of the damage they were doing to the environment. But in the absence of any other suggestions, they all felt, that they had to try this avenue, as they all knew that feeling sorry for themselves was not the right option. It was time for action.

Surely, there was no harm in trying, and transferring this virus could give them the chance they needed to get the humans to reflect on their devastating activities. The stifling air of uncertainty and silence amongst the participants only served to portray foggy and turbulent thoughts that all participants were pondering over in their minds. However, amidst the sorrow, dismay, fears, uncertainty, and anxiety; there was also an air of bewilderment on the practicality of task in hand, how this might be carried out and whether it will have any impact.

"Okay, that sounds like a plan," the Fox said rather loudly, to get all the animals out of that sultry, sad and uncertain mood and focus on the issue at hand.

The Lion who had been majestically sitting, quietly questioned, "The world is vast, and we are talking about reaching all humans all over the world, how is that possible?"

The Lion's outburst worked magic, as members' minds were diverted from the ambiguity and the uncertainty of their actions to focus on the practical aspects of transferring the virus from bats to humans and how they could spread from humans to humans, all over the world.

"Once the virus gets inside one human, spreading round the world would be easy," the Crow exclaimed with eagerness to see the execution of the idea.

Once again, mumbles and disquiet mainly focussed on

'how's' raged amongst the audience.

"How will the virus get inside the humans?"

"How will the bats transfer the virus to the humans?"

"How will it get transferred to all over the world?"

These were some of the myriads of questions that all in the congregation had. The stages of the virus passing from the bats to humans and its spread on a larger scale were difficult to conceive, contemplate or imagine.

"Well, we could use some of their very dirty habits like handling us alive before killing us for their food, to transfer the virus within us to them," the Bat said as he took control over his sad emotions.

"Yes, and once it is inside one human...." the Crow, wanting to be heard croaked excitedly. "Once the virus gets inside one human, their dirty habits of moving from one place to another, their lack of hygiene, shaking hands to greet each other, being in crowded places such as train stations, airports, and markets, will all help the virus to move from one person to another. Besides they travel all over the world in the name of progress, so they themselves can do our job of transferring the virus from human to human all over the world." The Crow was enjoying this forecast and its raised eyebrows were portraying its rather learned feelings.

"Will it stop the humans from destroying the environment?" the Wildebeest questioned. He wanted some assurance, as he had first-hand experience of the impacts of climate change and resulting draughts on the Serengeti Plains of Tanzania, his natural environment.

"Well," the Hen squeaked, making her point again, "when the virus inside me got to the humans, they did stop, took notice of how they were treating us, and made some changes in our environment". She added with an air of importance, "and I am sure that this virus would do the same."

"It is just that we do not want to harm the humans, just want them to stop, reflect and minimise the damage their activities are causing to the nature and all other living beings," the Dog cautioned, aware that the focus of all the animals now was on putting their plan into action and not any other consequences.

It was almost time for the conference to end, and there was the pressure for a decision and an outcome on the deliberation.

So the plot to transfer virus from the bats was hatched, all in the name of saving the world. In the name of making the humans reflect on their destructive activities that were damaging the environment. And in the name of the very Mother Earth that was nurturing them all!

Made by Indy Samra

A Series of Haiku

by Indy Samra

Life's Surprises

The journey of life,
Always twisting and turning.
Unknown surprises.

Maas Roti

Mother's roti,
Carefully prepared with love.
Best roti always.

Gratitude

Counting my blessings,
I look at all that I have.
I'm truly grateful.

Samay – Time

Samay, holli chal.
Eni kaali kadi aa?
Thora jeha tamm.

(Translated: Time, slow down.
What is the rush?
Stop for a short while.)

Maa Boli, Mother Tongue

by Indy Samra

Maa boli,
Spoken and inherited from our ancestors gone,
Our dharam, to maintain it for generations to come.
Our farz, to communicate in our maa boli.

Sadi pehchan:
Our identity.
Sadi shaan:
Our pride.

Maa boli,
Mother tongue.

Mere Naal Ehna Pyar? I am Loved

by Indy Samra

Mere Naal Ehna Pyar?
I am Loved.
Beloved Punjab was split into two.
My family could not take me with them.
Replaced by another, the love continued.

Mere Naal Ehna Pyar?
I am Loved.
Holding me in their hands, heartfelt gratitude is observed.
Being thankful for all that I grow.
Our connection is like no other.

Mere Naal Ehna Pyar?
I am Loved.
Birds above flying, singing their own tune in the air.
Children laugh, play, skip and run on the ground.
All around is filled with innocence, fun and freedom.

Mere Naal Ehna Pyar?
I am Loved.
The Secret meeting place for lovers.
In between tall, towering sugar canes or naturally crafted corn mazes.
Alone together, out sight.

Mere Naal Ehna Pyar?
I am Loved.
Handed down from generation to generation.

I have been taken care of and nurtured.
Being a substantial part of the family.

Mere Naal Ehna Pyar?
I am Loved.
Distance of thousands of miles has not separated us.
You have kept me in the hope of returning one day.
We will still have each other.

Mere Naal Ehna Pyar?
I am Loved.
Panjab's rich folk culture is my reflection.
Creativity at its finest.
Poetry, singing or dancing I am at the very essence of it.

Mere Naal Ehna Pyar?
I am Loved.
Daughter's wedding has been finalised.
I am looked at with hoped filled eyes.
Harvest that will be sold will make this occur.

Mere Naal Ehna Pyar?
I am Loved.
Proudly, my growth is shown to others.
Be it rice, wheat, herbs, vegetables or fruit.
Excitement beaming in the beholder's eyes.

Mere Naal Ehna Pyar?
I am Loved.
Through loudspeakers, reciting of prayers echo various times daily.
From Gurdwaras, Mandirs or Masjids.
Growing crops carry these vibrations within it.

Mere Naal Ehna Pyar?
I am Loved.
Believing in standing up for what is right.
Facing brutality and other injustices.
Yet you remain calm and always smile.

I look forward to your return and for us to progress together
as we always have done.

*Dedicated in support of the world's largest farmers protest in
history that has been taking place in India since November 2020
and continues today as I write this, 8th of February 2021.*

The Kindness Superheroes

by Indy Samra

Maahi and Maneet were tucked up in their bunk beds. Dad came in just as Mum finished reading the bedtime story.
He smiled at them both, "Goodnight you two, have an amazing sleep."
Mum started to close the bedroom door, "It's getting late so no chatting."
"Night, Mum; Night, Dad," they both said.

A few minutes later, Maahi put her bedside lamp on. Maneet came down the ladder of the bunk bed. They gave each other a high-five.
Maahi reaches for a shawl which is hanging on the bedroom door. This is no ordinary shawl; it has unique powers. It is a beautiful purple colour. Decorated in bright gems of different sizes and shapes, with silver and gold swirling printed patterns. Most superheroes have capes, but these superheroes have Mum's shawl. Long enough for both to hold onto at either end. They hold it behind them so it can help them fly, just like other superheroes capes do. Off they go.
Maahi and Maneet are Kindness Superheroes. Sharing kindness with other children - this is their quest. Lately there have been lots of changes for everyone, but the one thing that has not changed is being kind. The Kindness Superheroes leave a note. Each house Maahi and Maneet visit, they leave a note beside sleeping children with one sentence written on it. The children get to start the day with a smile after reading it. This is called an act of kindness. Here are some examples:

"I am amazing."

"My challenges have helped me grow."

"I am brave and strong."

"I am loved."

"I am beautiful."

"I am courageous."

"I treat others with kindness."

"I always do my best."

All the notes were delivered, except one.

"We seemed to have got around quickly tonight Maahi."

"Let's try that house over there Maneet."

As they quietly walk in the bedroom, they hear a soft calm voice.

"Who are you two? What are you doing here?"

Standing tall with her hands on her hips, "I am Maahi and this is Maneet. We are The Kindness Superheroes. What's your name?"

"My name is Dia."

Maneet smiles, "Great to meet you Dia, why are you still awake?"

Dia takes a deep sigh, "I was feeling a little sad today and I cannot sleep."

"We are sorry to hear this. It's a good job we visited today."

"Maneet," Maahi said, "Please give Dia the note we were going to leave for her. Dia, I would like you to read and repeat slowly four times what it says please."

Maneet passes Dia the note.

"I am the best, I am the best, I am the best, I am the best."

Dia stops and smiles.

"See how you start to tingle and feel nice when saying

nice things?" asks Maneet.

"Yes, I feel better, lighter and happier. I do not feel sad anymore. Thank you both."

"Our pleasure. The thing with kindness is we must be kind to ourselves and others too. Both are equally important and make us feel nice inside and out. It is simple. Be kind always." says Maahi. "You don't always have to leave notes to show kindness. You can smile at people you see, give compliments, do something nice for family and friends. Tell someone a joke or perhaps make a card for someone," explains Maneet.

"That's great. Thank you, but how can I be kind to myself?"

"I am glad you asked this Dia. You can do this by listening to a favourite song. Write or draw things that you are thankful for and that you like about yourself. Say some positive things whilst looking in the mirror. These are some of the things I say: I am perfect just the way I am. I am loved lots. I am ready to learn. I can do anything," shares Maneet.

"Wow, thank you. I'm definitely going to try this. I will be kind not just to others but to myself too!" says Dia excitedly.

"That's great to hear. Now close your eyes and try to sleep," says Maahi as they get ready to leave.

The Kindness Superheroes did great at delivering the messages and having a talk with Dia. Making their way back home, flying in the magnificent star-lit sky. They both enjoyed spreading kindness; it made them feel wonderful.

So, remember kindness is niceness. Share compassion always with everyone.

As Dolly Parton has quoted, "if you see someone without a smile give them one of yours."

Why don't you try writing some of your own notes for your family and for yourself?

(Maneet requested that the Dolly Parton quote be added at the end of the story.)

Bhangra Queen
by Indy Samra

The late 1980's and early 1990's saw the birth of British-Asian bhangra music. Music my mum would play on cassettes in the car. Records Dad would play at the weekend, whilst having a few cheeky Whiskeys. Music I would listen to with my friends. East meets West creativity through music. Bhangras popularity rocketed, especially with the second-generation British-Asians like me.

Just after my 16th birthday, my best friend Kiran was telling me about how she and her sister, Sharon, had snuck out to a Bhangra gig.

"The next gig is coming up in a weeks' time, ask your parents if you can come to ours for a sleepover Taj? we can go," said Kiran excitedly.

"Sleepover and sneak out! You crazy!? Would your parents not wake up with us three creeping around the house, Kiran?"

The shear thought of doing this sent a shiver of fear down my spine.

"Nah; Dads snores his head off. Mum is tired too, so she'll be knocked out as well."

"Damn, Kiran - wish my parents would deep-sleep like that. If I sneeze in my bedroom at night and my mum will say she heard me the next day."

"Not my parents, Taj, they have no idea. We have sneaked downstairs and watched TV in the dark with volume on low before. Channel 4 put them Bollywood movies on so late on a school night. They must think us Asians don't sleep," said Kiran.

"Yeah, Shaan was on the other week at 1am. Mum made me set up the VCR to record it."

I could not concentrate in maths lesson. Mr Brown had this dull tone in his voice that just makes me lose interest at the best of times. Today I had my own debate going on in my head.

"Should today be the day I ask my parents about the sleep over?"

That evening, after Roti, I plucked up the courage and asked if I could stay the night round Kiran's house on a school night to complete some homework.

Mum and Dad looked at each other before Dad replied, "Haa, teek aa, Tajinder."

I felt like pinching myself. Did Dad really say yes? Never mind Cinderella going to the ball, Taj is going to go to a Bhangra gig! What would I wear? how would I do my hair? Yikes how exciting!

The night of the sleepover had arrived.

"See you tomorrow after school Mum," I said as I picked up my extra heavy school bag.

"Gal sun Tajinder, be a nice guest at Kiran's house," Mum said this in true Panjabi style. One hand on her hip and with the other hand in mid-air waving the index finger whist taking.

"Hanji, Mum, see you tomorrow."

Auntieji had prepared a lovely meal for us.

"Taj, hor roti leh."

"Thank you for the offer, Auntieji, but I'm okay."

Even though I probably could have managed another one, but I had started to feel nervous about what we had planned.

"Kurriyoh, complete your homework before going to bed.

I'm going back into the shop," Auntieji said.

"Taj, try this red lipstick on. It will look great with the black and gold sequin top," said Kiran.

It was nine thirty and the three of us were ready. Kiran switched the cassette off. We always liked to listen to the album *Ishq* by the Sahotas.

"We will have to get in bed and switch the lights off before ten as Mom and Dad will be coming upstairs shortly after. The cab is booked to pick us up at the end of the street at eleven," Sharon said.

Lights out, fully dressed with a face full of makeup, I was shitting myself and excited at the same time. Under the duvet I was being careful not to rub my face. I was not worried about the pink eye shadow or the black eyeliner smudging. I was more worried about staining the sheets and leaving evidence for Auntyji to find.

I could hear footsteps coming up the stairs. Uncleji yawned very loud as he walked past our room. I could hear Auntieji's bangles jingle as she lifted her hand to switch the landing light off, click.

All I could feel was my heart drumming a beat in my chest. The feelings of bravery were gradually creeping in. Prior, I had been thinking of how disappointed our parents would be if we got caught.

Kiran got up and slowly opened the bedroom door. She paused, then indicated to me and Sharon to follow her. Kiran had already said to follow her exact steps, as she knew where the floorboards and stairs creaked. I paused and tried not to laugh at the loud sound of Uncleji's snoring. Not paying attention, I stepped on the wrong spot on the stairs. Oh shit.

Both girls looked at me and we all froze. As I slightly moved my foot, the step creaked a little more. Oh my God, what do I do? Hiyo rabba.

After a few seconds - which seemed to have lasted an eternity - we could still hear Uncleji snoring. We carried on and made our way down the stairs and into the kitchen.

Sharon picked up the biscuit tin. No biscuits; however, plenty of savoury snacks. A regular occurrence in most south-Asian households. The empty Christmas biscuit tins usually stored Mattari and Seerni. The spare back-door key lay at the bottom of the tin.

We needed comfy shoes to run down the street. So we put on our plain flat ones. Plus, Auntyji would have thought it was odd that we were wearing heals to school. These Panjabi Mums should be working for the CID under-cover - they do not really miss a thing. Hence, such careful planning and preparation had gone into sneaking out. Sharon put the key in the door and starts to turn it. The mass cluster of butterflies in my tummy were fluttering around like they could hear the song 'Chan Mere Makhna' by Balwinder Safri. Any second now, would Auntieji make a dramatic entrance, waving her arms in the air shouting 'Nahi!', with Uncleji following closely behind with wide blood shot raging eyes?

The cold weather did not seem to bother us as we raced towards the end of the street.

"We got five minutes till the taxi comes, girls," Sharon said.

I was stood thinking, what if Kiran's parents have woken up and realised we were not home? What if they call my parents? What if they come out looking for us and see us at the end of the street?

I soon forgot these questions as the taxi pulled up.

"Black Orchid nightclub please," Sharon says.

We did it! We've escaped! The three of us were thrilled and eager about being on our way to our night out. Achanak and Sat Rang would performing, as well as The Sahotas. We had seen them all perform previously at weddings and at the outdoor mela's. But today was going to be a new experience. We could see crowds outside the club as we got closer.

"It's packed. We will never get in," Kiran said.

There just seemed to be people everywhere. We got out the taxi, trying to work out where the end of the queue was. Looking around, I spotted someone my older brother knows just staring at me. I quickly turned my back to him. But the next minute I felt him breathing down my neck, so I turned around and smiled.

"Hello Taj, what you are doing here?"

Don't you just hate it when someone asks you this when you are both at the same place.

"You won't get in; tickets are all sold out. People including myself have been waiting ages to get in."

I say goodbye to him as Sharon pulls my arm. She'd spotted someone she knew and wanted to avoid. We stood at the side of the club, away from the crowd at the main entrance. Just then a fire door flung open wide. A drunk guy practically fell out, stumbling around. I looked at the girls and told them to follow me. Impulsively, I led the way. It was not like I was regularly doing this sort of thing, but my intuition at that precise moment told me to go through the open door.

We ran though the corridor, the muffled music was getting louder and clearer the closer we were getting.

"You nutter, Taj! That was quick thinking, love it!" said Kiran.

We came to another door, but we unquestionably knew from the clear sounds that the inside of the club was on the other side. I had never seen anything like it. The place was packed. Big bright flashing lights and sounds bouncing off the walls!

We headed straight to the dancefloor which was over-spilling to the seating areas. You could not move. Bhangra dancing on the spot was a first. We got pushed and shoved a little but that was to be expected.

The stage was crammed too, with live musicians and singers. This was a proper live set. Dhol, tabla, tumbi, couple of guitarists, big synthesisers, and not forgetting drum kits. The singers had crazy mullets and were wearing bright colours full of glittery sequins. They made me look like a plain-jane in comparison. They were singing their hearts out on stage.

It was an awesome night. We decided to take a little walk around. Everyone was having a good time. Girls doing the usual - carefully inspecting from head to toe what other girls were wearing. Guys in their little crews swarming around groups of girls. Drunks are always funny to watch. Couples canoodling up in corners who clearly needed to just get a room.

I was wondering how many others have sneaked out. Most looked a little older than us. Perhaps they were at university, away from home. Coaches from other cities universities travelled Bhangra gigs. The lengths these bhangra fans must've gone to! So many Asians, the same generation in one place, wow. You had the odd Uncleji / Auntyji in the club, but it was cool, as we did not know them.

Dancing away, I felt on tap on my shoulder. Looking up I was mesmerised by how handsome this chap was, with the most charming smile too.

He was dancing on a podium along with a few other people. Holding his hand out he invited me to join him. Placing my hand into his, he elegantly pulled me up next to him. This was something out of a Bollywood movie.

As I look dreamily into his big hazel eyes, I feel we should have had some violins playing in the background with Lata Mangeshkar's voice gently humming. Were we going to be happily ever after, or would an evil villain appear? That made me think of my brother's acquaintance I saw earlier. Was he inside now watching me from a distance?

(Anyway, let's not ruin the moment talking about him, back to my hero.)

We were dancing quite close to one another. We didn't have much space; cannot say I was complaining though.

Gently putting his fingers in my hair, he moved this away from my ear and leaning forward even closer he asks me my name.

"My name is Tajinder, but most people call me Taj, what's your name?"

He chuckles. "My name is Rajinder, I prefer to be called Raj."

We came from the generation where most Panjabi names ended with inder, jit, preet or deep. To confuse matters more, most names were unisex names too. Bet the predominantly-white teachers in schools loved trying to memorise names and faces. Had a nice ring to it though, Raj and Taj.

My mind started to drift. I pictured our wedding invitations. Rajinder weds Tajinder. The sound of the saxophone soon brought me back as Sat Rang started to perform Dhola veh Dhola. I loved this song, and to be sharing this dance with Raj was memorable. The pungent, aromatic, woody smell of his aftershave was divine. Certainly, wasn't Brut 33.

Dancing away I was having an incredible time. Kiran and Sharon were near me on the dancefloor. They were full of smiles too. It was an unforgettable night. Looking around all I could see were happy people having a great time. Bhangra gigs - this was what all the fuss was about, and I was at one experiencing it for myself.

The lights came on and a slow Panjabi song was being sung. Musicians started packing instruments away. Subtle hint that it was almost time to go.

Raj gave me his hand and helped me off the podium.

"It was really nice to meet you Taj, hopefully see you again at the next gig," Raj said as he was putting his black leather jacket on.

"Really nice meeting you too Raj. Yeah, hopefully see you again soon".

"You going to be alright getting home?"

"Yes I will be fine, thanks for asking."

"Take care Taj."

Raj gave me a big bear hug wrapping his arms around me. Then he held my face in his hands and kissed my forehead. Ever have those moments where you wish time could just stop for a while? This was one of those moments. I stood at the edge of the dance floor watching Raj go off with his friends. He did look back and we exchanged one more smile.

"Come on, Bhangra queen, let's go flag a taxi," Sharon told me.

And the three of us started to head for the main exit.

"Thanks for tonight girls, I've had an epic time. Loved it."

"That's ok; anytime ,Taj. We can always go again," Kiran said.

The clock in the taxi said 3:10 AM. Sharon made sure the taxi dropped us away from the house.

"Put all the clothes in the bin liner that's at the bottom of the wardrobe. They stink of cigarettes. I will put them onto wash when Mum's not around. Next to the bin liner is a box of face wipes. Use these to remove make-up and put these in the bin bag too," Sharon said.

Creeping down the dark passageway to the kitchen door I was feeling nervous again, just like when we were leaving earlier.

Kiran gently puts the key in and turns the lock. Will Uncleji and Auntieji be stood behind the door? Even worse, will *my* parents be standing with them?

Phew! The coast was clear. I followed Kiran's exact footsteps this time. Uncleji was snoring still.

I lay in bed, reflecting on the extraordinary evening and the fact we didn't get caught. I could not help wondering if I will ever see Raj again.

The next thing I knew was the sound of the curtains opening and day light coming in.

"Utto kurriyoh. You will be late for school," Auntieji said.

Walking thoughts

by Indy Samra

I tie up my shoelaces to my trainers. I feel that the *Rocky* movie theme should be playing in the background. Today is a new challenge for me: walking 10,000 steps a day for ten days. It's a fundraising challenge for Midlands Langar Seva Society. Till now, I had not really counted my daily steps.

With my hot pink lipstick on and matching-coloured headphones, off I go. The cold, crisp autumn weather and wet slippery leaves beneath my feet at Victoria Park, Leicester is not going to stop me.

I see lots of faces. Some smile back, some don't. The odd few even greet me with a 'good morning' and a short conversation. Everyone is at the park for different reasons, I guess. Using it as a short cut to get somewhere, to walk the dog, do daily exercise or as a meeting place.

I reach for my phone and shuffle the playlist on Spotify. Gosh, gone are the days of Sony Walkman's and cassettes. At the touch of a button, I have an array of music. 'Mausam pyar ka' plays, an 80s Hindi cinema song. It isn't the weather for love; I put my cold hands in my coat pocket.

Walking along made me realise how much walking my dear dad used to do. He had a rare condition of rheumatoid arthritis and was diagnosed when he was in his early 30s. Even with his disability, I am sure he probably walked more than 10,000 steps a day at least a couple of times a week.

Grabbing a sandwich Mum had made and his bottle of water, off he'd go. Meeting with his friend at Derby bus station, they would walk together to the Indian community centre, spend a few hours there and then walk back. That walk must have been a few miles, I'm sure. He never let his disability get the better of him. He would push himself harder and harder. He had willpower and determination as well as self-discipline. For the next ten days I must keep the same mindset.

Just then the 'Rail Gaddi' starts to play. What a tune! No Panjabi get-together is complete without doing the conga to this. It brings a smile to my face. I look around, but no one is close enough for me to grab. Probably a good thing.

Instead, I step up and walk a little faster. This song alone must be at least 1000 steps. Maybe I should pop it on repeat and do a few more laps around the park.

Paare hojao saare, Indy di rail gaddi ayi.

The Healing Oak Tree Meditation
by Indy Samra

For the next few minutes, take some time to relax the body and mind.

Begin by taking some nice deep breaths. Gradually fill your lungs with air and when you are ready, fully release that breath out. Slowly, emptying your lungs fully.

Then continue to breathe slowly, deeply and gently, at your own natural pace and rhythm.

With each breath you take, your thoughts become lighter.

Allow the gentle movement of your breath to guide you into an even more relaxed state.

Allow images to form in your mind naturally in your own time.

In front of you is a closed gate. You open this and step through onto a path.

The path is made of singular smooth pebbles of all different colours and sizes. As you start to walk, your feet make a crunching sound on the stones.

The heat of the sun warms you from head to toe.

The path in front starts to bend around a corner and you feel excited. What will you see when you turn the corner?

As you turn, in front of you at the end of the path is a big oak tree. Walking towards the tree, you can hear the birds singing. The soft sounds of nature fill your ears. A gentle breeze warmly touches you. You are at peace and all around you is calm and tranquil.

You feel a gentle pull guiding you towards the big oak tree. It's standing so strong. In all weathers, it survives due to the strength and endurance it has.

Approaching the oak tree, notice how big and dark the trunk is. It is almost black. Your run your fingers gently over the ridges, stroking them lovingly. Caressing them.

Looking up, notice the crown of the oak tree. It has sturdy branches with shiny dark-green leaves. The leaves rustle, making a swishing sound.

Branches tenderly sway, almost dancing in rhythm with the gentle breeze.

The heat of the sun filters through to you between the branches and leaves.

Turning your back to the tree, you lean up against it. Softly closing your eyes, standing strong and tall just like the oak tree.

Roots start to grow from the soles of your bare feet, growing in all directions beneath the soil, interweaving with the roots from the oak tree.

From the oak tree's roots, golden healing energy is being released.

You pull this golden healing energy through into your roots. The healing energy slowly continues to move up into your feet, making its way gradually to your ankles, moving on up to the knees, up to the thighs, up to the abdominal area, moving around to your lower back, then upper back, moving around to the chest area, continuing up to the shoulders and down both arms to the fingertips. Then back up your arms to your neck, up to your face, eyes, forehead and to the top of your head.

Take some slow deep breaths, and let the healing energy radiate through your whole body. Abundantly giving you the healing that you need.

Slowly untangle your roots and release them from the oak tree's. Your own roots gradually grow back up through the ground. Up, up reaching the soles of your feet and vanishing.

Taking a deep breath, you gently let the sunlight into your eyes by slowly opening them.

You give thanks to the oak tree for the shelter it provided and for immersing you from head to toe with its healing energy.

It is time you headed back. Slowly you start to walk back up the path.

The smooth, colourful pebbles make a crunching sound as you tenderly place your feet on them.

As you're about to turn the corner towards the open gate, you look back and admire the Healing Oak Tree. Today's healing has been truly valuable.

As you continue to walk to the gate you smile.

You close the gate behind you, knowing in your heart you can return to the Healing Oak Tree whenever you need to.

Made by Nutan Dattani-Patel

Breath of Fresh Air

by Nutan Dattani-Patel

For each breath of life
What price for the air?
Did we care?
Did we really care?
That fresh air, so vital
So clean, so fresh, necessary for life,
Did we care?
Did we really care?
It took a virus to taint the air
We suffered, we lost
Will we care,
Will we really care?

Eternal Love

by Nutan Dattani-Patel

Father and daughter.
Special bond of love and joy.
Blissful Happiness!

Ji Lo

by Nutan Dattani-Patel

Khayal Aaj Mooje Aaya
Duniya Kuch Bhi Kahe Aur Soche
Jina Muje Aajhi he!

Mother and Me

by Nutan Dattan-Patel

Mother given birth
Rewarded with a daughter
Reflection of 'Me'

Reflection of the Pandemic

by Nutan Dattani-Patel

I was told I cried with my first breath of air
So vital, so pure, then I forgot about the air
Nature around me took the same
But it gave back more than its share
It knew the game and I did not care

In 2020 Coronavirus came to play in the air
Camouflaged and laid itself bare
For us to breathe its deadly ware
Into our lungs it stayed to despair
Now we started to declare
We are the ones who should care
The one vital necessity for our life: the clean air

We now have time to reflect for a whole year
To take care of OUR air!

First Love

by Nutan Dattani-Patel

My life started with you
You were my very first love
My Papa, it was just me and you.

Every time I fell, you cried too
You lifted me and treated me like a dove
My Papa, it was just me and you.

When at school, I had no clue
You always taught me to learn tough
That same belief of me and you.

When I grew, I believed in you
Always with me whenever I rove
My Papa, it was just me and you .

Now I nest away from you
A whole life nurtured with love
I call on you to give me your view.

Years of love saw me through
But now I yearn for you above
My life started with you
My Papa, it was just me and you.

Made by Usha Patel

The Beach

by Sangeeta Rajput

Dreaming of a day at the beach.
Walking hand-in-hand along the promenade,
Watching the sea move in and out.
Eating fish and chips made fresh that day.
Chasing my brother into the sea.

Dreaming of a day at the beach.
Playing on the arcade machines, flashing lights and sounds.
Collecting shells left along the sand.
Watching the sea move in and out.
Flying seagulls swooping down.
Children building sandcastles.

Dreaming of a day at the beach
Candyfloss galore, ice creams: 99p, feast and more.
Riding a donkey across the sand.
Watching the sea move in and out.
Seeing the lighthouse along the skyline.
Wishing time would stand still so I can breathe the sea air.
Watching the sea move in and out.

Dad

by Sangeeta Rajput

My heart aches to see you walk through the door.
I miss you teasing me about my hair, my new shoes.
How I want you to smile at me
To make me chicken curry, have a beer.
I watched you fall asleep on the sofa.
I teased you and woke you up.
I did it because I was scared.

The day you left will never be forgotten.
You stayed in my heart; you are alive in my thoughts.
At every important event you are there.
Miss my hero, my Dad.

You remain with me till the day I die.

Love Sangeeta xx

Mummy's Story

by Sangeeta Rajput

When I woke up this morning, for a moment thought I was
thirty again. Getting ready for my flight to Milan, beginning
my birthday celebrations... Instead, I was met by the sound of
my baby crying for the tenth time.

How life has changed in the last decade, when angels took
my dad away. Mum became ill, and my brother got married,
as did I. Life moves on, but we remain lost in our memories.

How I wanted to remain asleep, with the beautiful
memories entwined in my dreams. I smiled, remembering the
fun we had in Milan. All the food we ate, the sights we saw. I
sink my head into the pillow, as if a loved one was holding me
tight. I can't seem to move my body, as if I have surrendered
myself to my bed. This is where I wanted to be - together
with my thoughts.

"Hurry up," shouted a voice inside.

I quickly got ready. We were late - so much to do. I
rushed to the bathroom, grabbed the toothbrush and brushed
my teeth as I shower. The things we do to save time. I ran
to my son, Max's room and got him ready to go to the day-
nursery. He was not impressed with Mummy's multi-tasking
skills pulling and prodding him left, right and centre.

I entered the kitchen, drinking my tea while getting
breakfast ready. My son looks in horror as his porridge is
made. He stared in shock at the finished article, then pushed
the bowl away and pointed to the toast on my plate. No time
for this game; 'porridge is what you'll eat.' After a lot of
pushing and shoving, breakfast was done.

Grabbing my keys and bag, I put my son in his car-seat. I

took a deep breath, gritting my teeth, and started the car.

Off we go.

The drive to the nursery was a time for me to listen to my favourite tunes. Max was happy gazing out of the window, watching cars drive by, yelling out the colours in excitement.

We arrive at the nursery. Time to hand my son over and save my sanity.

"There you go Janine, take Max - he is itching to play."

Max looked back at me, as if to say, 'off you go; I want to play.'

I feel a sense of relief - time to get things done. But I want to sleep.

I return to the house and see the pile of clothes for ironing. My heart sinks and my hands clam up. I look up the stairs and feel my bed calling me, then look back to the clothes...

My head hits the soft pillow and I wrap my tired body with the duvet, closing my eyes to the world so I can dream again. The chores can wait. The mind floats away as I enter the dream world.

Made by Shahida Ravaliya

A Tribute to My Dad

by Ela Chauhan

I am the person I am today because of my parent's unconditional love and their devotion to their family. My dad loved mine and Jagruti's food. We made him dokhla, patra and home-made vegetarian food. It was such a pleasure to see his face light up like the sun. He said the food reminded him of my mum's cooking.

I treasure our memories together. My parents helped to raise my children. Devina was born first and then Dharmesh. They spoilt them rotten! They were such proud grandparents. I owe them such a debt of gratitude for helping me to raise them into the fine individuals they are today. My children's success is theirs.

On one memorable trip, Raju and I were planning a holiday to India. My dad was so excited to join us. To my surprise, he planned a trip to every temple he had wanted to visit with my mum but was unable to. We visited Powergar, Ranchodji mandir in Dakor and Siddhi Vinayak temple. He said that you could only visit these places according to the time of god's wishes, and not before that. It was a dream of mine and his to visit those temples. It was made so much more special with my dad next to me.

My parents worked day and night to provide for us. I still remember making chapatis with my mum. We took pride in making it perfect - only to see my dad guzzle them up with his curry!

Mum left us five years ago and my dad filled her shoes as both parents. I've learnt so much about my heritage and culture from him. My faith in god comes from my parents.

I'll carry on these traditions forever, passing them onto the next generation, Evalina, your beautiful great-granddaughter, I am so glad they met her. I remember him kissing her and remarking how pretty she was. He called her his 'mini Devina'. I hope she inherits his smile and heart of gold.

My husband, Raju, came here from India. Dad welcomed him as a son. They shared the same passions: drinking and cricket. Raju'd always find my dad in the Indian Queen, enjoying few drinks with friends.

My dad helped me to buy my first home. It's become a house of wonderful memories. Every time I look at the garden, I see him with a pint in his hand and paneer sizzler, enjoying one of Raju's barbecue with the family. I hear Dad's laughter ringing in my ears and see his smile every time I close my eyes.

Every day after work, I would drink Dad's home-made speciality: masala tea. If I didn't call him, he would ring me and say, *"dikra aje tu gare ne avi"* (you did not come home to see me). I'll miss those visits. But I'll remember him every time I drink some tea.

Dad's last wishes for his children was to stay positive in the face of life's struggles. He said to concentrate on your inner strength, and god will be with you to the end.

To my darling parents, thank you for the wonderful journey we shared together. Your blessings and teachings will remain with me forever. Dad, you fought till the end. Your legacy will continue through your children.

Love you always. You are both reunited.

Jai Sri Krishna.

BE
BLESSED
ALWAYS

Made by Kaulshalia Chudasama

Learning English as a Second Language
by Ranjan Saujani

"She was here only a moment ago, that Indira. Where has she gone?" said Mrs Brown, the English teacher taking the class register.

She looked around, as did all the adult students who had come to learn English.

It was only the second session of the course, and it seemed as if the students were still trying to acquaint with each other. They all sat there, quiet, attentive to the "Guru", the teacher. The women were dressed in their traditional saris with thick sweaters on. Some had scarves round their heads, tied tight with a knot under the chins, covering the ears. The three male students had their jackets and coats still on, with one wearing a woolly hat and gloves.

The windy September weather, sitting in a cold church room, with only one radiator, wasn't warm enough for all these new arrivals from India, Uganda and Pakistan.

"Okay, let's start today's lesson," said Mrs Brown. "We have two new students joining us today. Hello," she went over to one of the female students. "My name is Mrs Brown. What is your name?"

The student stood up, looking very puzzled, almost frightened that she had been picked on.

"You don't have to stand up," said Mrs Brown and repeated her sentence, this time speaking louder and slower, stressing each word loudly.

How typical to assume that if someone is struggling to understand what you are saying, they might understand if you speak louder.

The student kept standing up, and said hesitantly, "No, Madam, you are not brown, I am brown.... you Mrs White and me Mrs Brown!"

The students broke into a loud laughter.

"Quite everyone!" said Mrs Brown, "No, no, no, My name is Mary Brown" she said exasperated, "What is.......?"

She did not finish her sentence as all the students were laughing and talking amongst themselves.

Mrs Brown looked at her register, to remind herself of the new student's name. "Ok, repeat after me. Say, 'My name is Santok Patel.'"

Mrs Patel was more confused. "No Madam, why you confuse me? First you say your name is Mrs Brown, now you say your name is Santok Patel?"

Mrs Patel put her hand over her forehead, more confused, exasperated. She sat down heavily on her chair, while the rest of the class was roaring in laughter.

Mrs Brown was finding it difficult to control the class; some people were laughing, others were talking in their own language which she couldn't understand........

Just then, Indira walked in through the open door. She started walking towards the only empty chair, next to a male student, then dragging the chair to the side where all the women were sitting.

"Where have you been, Indira? " said Mrs Brown, following Indira's movement across the room.

"Madam I went to my home to get my notebook. I forget my book, I come to class in a hurry… Too much to do before I come to learn English. Husband wants hot chappatis every day, children coming home for lunch... and... and..."

"That's okay, Indira, don't worry; sit down. Next time, if

you forget your notebook, I will give you some paper to write on, so don't go running home."

"So, Madam, you won't hit me with a stick on my hand, if I forget? My teacher in my town in India, he used to hit us. Very painful," she said, looking at her palms, remembering the pain she must have endured in her childhood.

"No. of course not. Now sit down, Indira. Let's carry on," said Mrs Brown, turning around to write on the blackboard.

Varsha and Mina, the two younger women in the class, were sitting next to each other. Their age and university background was something they had in common. All the older students in the room might have attended only school years in India. Jaya had a BA degree in Sanskrit and Mina had a BA degree in Home Economics. They couldn't understand why they had been put in the beginners' English class. They could understand English well, except for the different ways people used the language in England. They all spoke so differently compared to the BBC World Service's English they were used to hearing in India. Jaya had been in this country 6 months; Mina had been here for about nine. Both were newly married to Indian boys from the UK, trying to adjust to living with their new extended families, a new culture and cold weather.

"Jaya, this teacher could be compared to a good Sasuji, would you say?" whispered Mina, in Gujarati.

"What do you mean, Mina?"

"Well she calls out people's names without regard to their ages and their experiences. Why doesn't she have respect for the older students in our class? 'Jaya', 'Indira', 'Manjula'… She calls them like my mother-in-law, exercising her own older status as a Sasuji. Our people in this class are all older than Mrs Brown. But instead of giving them due respect by calling them 'Manjulaben' or 'Santokben' or 'Jamanbhai' or 'Indiraben', like we should do, she calls them as if they are children, with no experience in life. How very rude, no respect for elders." Mina paused, remembering her own schooling experience in India. "But Mrs Brown would be a good Sasu too. At least she won't be a strict person and use a cane."

"Today, we are going to talk about directions," said Mrs Brown, raising her voice to gain attention. She drew arrows on the blackboard."This is going to the left… and this arrow is pointing towards the right. Now I want you all to write in your books how you come to English class from your home. So, write 'Home' at the top of the page and then write how many left or right turns you have to make to come to class…" Mrs Brown sensed puzzlement on the students' faces as they stared at the board. "Okay, let me explain. Jaman, tell me, how did you come to class from your home, today?"

"See, rude again!" whispered Mina, "how can you call an older man by his name only?! No manners."

Jaya nodded in agreement but dare not put her agreement in words, due to respect for a teacher. A teacher's words, in her culture, you should never oppose.

Jamanbhai got up from his seat to reply. "Madam, my home on Hury-son road."

"No, not 'Hury son'. It's Harrison Road." corrected Mrs Brown.

"No Madam, we live on Hury-son Road. When we first come to Leicester, I could not remember the name of my road. So my son, he very clever in English. He says, 'Bapuji, just remember, you are the son of Hari. Hari means God, you see! So you say Hury-son. I am so lucky. I say to myself, I am God's son.' So nice, na?". He turned

round, looking for approval from other student.
They all nodded and smiled in agreement. "Wah! wah!
How auspicious! so fortunate. God's son, wah, wah."
"Okay, okay, let's get back to 'directions', said Mrs
Brown, not quite sure whether to agree with him or not.
She was taken aback by the approval and agreement
from all the students, and by the verbal and non-verbal
communication in the class. Maybe she felt it was
undermining her teaching methods. "Let's get back to our
topic. Jaman, how did you come to class from your home
today?"
Mina raised her eyebrows and shook her head in disbelief,
"She'll never learn." she said under her breath.
"Ok, Madam," started Jamanbhai, "I come out of my
house. I turn right. I walk, walk, I come to Melton Road.
I turn left. I walk, walk, walk long way, I come to the
Church. And my class upstairs in the Church."
"Very good, Jaman." she said. "Now class, I want you to
do the same. How do you, come to class? Write in your
books."

At this point Mina couldn't take it anymore. She slapped
her pen on her open notebook in a silent protest. In her view,
the insult of Jamanbhai was too much.

The students started writing busily. Mrs Brown looked
at her watch. Not long to go before the end of the session.
Perhaps she will give one bit of feedback, then give the
homework and finish the class, she was planning in her mind.
She will come more prepared next time, she thought.

After about five minutes, Mrs Brown said, "Right
everyone, who wants to go first and tell us how they come
to class?"
Nobody volunteered.
"Shampa, why don't you tell us?"

Everyone started laughing at Mrs Brown. Not knowing what was going on, Mrs Brown walked up to the older woman sitting in the second row. The woman looked terrified.

At this point, Mina, not being able to curtail herself anymore, stood up. "Madam, excuse me. Her name is not 'Shampa', its Champa. And we all call her Champaben because she is older than us."

This reaction shocked Mrs Brown. She took some time to think. "Okay, we haven't got much time. Would you like to tell us…?" She looked at Champaben, not daring to say her name.

Champaben stood up to answer the teacher. She hesitated, shook her head, then put her right hand on her forehead, gesturing how difficult this task was for her.

"Madam, this very difficult for me, you know. It give me headache," she said patting her forehead. "Turn right, turn left, turn right....... I don't know how to come here. My husband bring me here, I follow my husband. I don't look at right or left. So you ask my husband when he comes. He tell you how to come."

Writer's note: These are some of the true incidents and experiences of newly arrived Asian adults (and their teachers) in Leicester when they go to learn English as a second language.

Day Out Of Lockdown

by Ranjan Saujani

I have been shielding from the pandemic since March 2020.
Due to my age and underlying medical conditions, I had been
put in a clinically vulnerable category by the NHS. What does
that really mean in reality? Well, I have spent all of the last
year with my husband (who is also in this category), at home,
isolating myself even from my children and grandchildren. No
family Diwali celebrations, no Christmas get-togethers and no
hugging babies - who have now grown into toddlers. The only
perk for us was getting a priority slot at Tesco's for online
shopping!

After staying home through the whole of last summer,
autumn and winter, the 'Government's road-map out of
lockdown' raised a lot of hope. But when the Government
finally said that up to six people would be allowed to meet
outside in the park, I had a lot of doubt. Would this really
happen in Leicester? Could this really happen in Leicester?
Leicester has never been out of lockdown, even for short
periods, like other places in the country. We have had the
longest period of lockdown in the country and the instances of
Covid 19 are still high in some parts of the city. Was it really
safe to go out?

When Monday 29th of March finally arrived, the biggest
shock was learning that Leicester had partially lifted the
lockdown with the rest of the country. Unfortunately for both
the Government and health officials, the day turned out to be
a gloriously sunny - the first warm day after the dark days of
winter.

We decided to go to the open spaces in Abbey Park. When

we arrived, the carpark was full, so we had to park further away. Loads of people in bright summer clothes were heading towards the park gates. It seemed as if fashion had changed overnight - the shorts and t-shirts, the sunglasses. There were people with outdoor games and footballs in their hands; groups of families and friends were moving towards the open spaces by the river.

The afternoon sun was shining, the trees were a lush green, and some of the bushes had bloomed with early spring flowers. There was an air of happiness all around. The fountain in the middle of the small lake seemed to be singing to the tunes of the visitors. Families had laid blankets and mats down for picnics. Children were running round excitedly, laughing and enjoying the free spaces after having been confined at home for such a long time. Some babies and toddlers were probably out in the sunshine for the first time, and you could see their hesitation and discomfort with the bright sunlight.

The young people, a lot of them in shorts and t-shirts, were playing football, badminton and other ball games. So many people out with their dogs. Most older people were sitting on benches enjoying this beautiful day. And yet there was something more in the air - the laughter, the happiness and most of all, that sense of freedom. People were polite to each other, exchanging 'Good afternoon' to strangers, there were smiles of gratefulness and a sense of relief on people's faces.

A long year of social distancing from people seemed no-more. People seemed to be glad to see other people, celebrating life, human company, and freedom from the fear of the dreaded Corona virus.

Made by Rozmin Watson

When Dreams Come True
by Sonia Thompson

Alison wipes her sweaty palms down her thighs, her bright eyes dart around the room. Above her the stage lights illuminate a chubby frame, rosy cheeks and a shock of red hair that has been tamed into a makeshift bun with the assistance of gel, hairpins and a handful of elastic bands, stolen from the school office. She taps her feet in frustration and anticipation as she awaits the opening chords that will mark out the beginning of her first major musical performance.

The soft whispers from early onlookers indicate that they are surprisingly impressed by her immaculate costume and bright red dancing shoes.

"Is that Alison Pickford?" It sounded like Jamie Darcey. He seemed confused.

"Yeah – she looks kinda good," his friend whispered.

A broad smile spreads across the Alison's face, as she remembers rushing home a few weeks ago to share some earth-shattering news.

"Mum, Mum, where are you?" she had yelled, tossing her school bag onto a pile of dirty, worn-out shoes in the hallway. Shoes that would have been designated for the trash in any other household, but the one in which she resided.

The kitchen door had opened to reveal a short unassuming woman, dressed in a variety of polyester materials with clashing polka dots, stripes and zigzags with no unifying colours. Usually, Alison would sigh whenever she saw her mum's poorly-dressed figure approaching, but not today.

Instead, she had looked past the clothes that epitomised a scarecrow version of the 'before image' observable in a myriad of advertising miracle makeovers. There were far more important matters at hand.

"What is it Alison? What's the noise all about?" her mum asked, wiping her hands on a kitchen towel.

"Guess," demanded Alison, skipping around the room in delight.

"What, what is it? Alison Pickford, you're not in any trouble, are you?" Her mother's eyes narrowed, her voice accusatory and tense, squeezing at the corners of her larynx and making her voice rise in pitch.

Alison dodged her mother's grasp to playfully grab some biscuits from the coffee table. She glanced at the jobs section of the newspaper, and thought briefly of dad upstairs in the bedroom, paralysed by self-loathing and depression.

"Tsk, don't be silly, Mum. You know I never get in trouble. That would take somebody to notice me in the first place. Anyway, it's good news," she said, leaning against the wall as she pushed the sweet crumbly treat into her mouth.

Her mother flopped herself down in the nearest sofa, and for the first time she smiled. The chair was old and covered in dog hairs, with dark stains that no one had been able to wash away. An inheritance from grandma, who regularly reminded them that they 'had been lucky to get it.'

"Well, is it something to do with your grades, or what about that nice young m-?" her mother looked off into the distance.

She jumped to her feet, "I got the part. The main part," Alison said before her mother could finish her sentence, "And Bob Filtchett is nobody's idea of a nice young man – urgh."

Crumbs splattered their way down the front of Alison's white school blouse onto the carpet. She hesitated briefly, glimpsing the mess at her feet, before bouncing over to give her mum an enormous cuddle, and the two of them jumped up and down until her Mum begged her to stop and returned to the old brown sofa to catch her breath.

Today however, here on the stage, Alison's young knees reveal a tremor as the introductory notes from the piano rise from beneath her. She hums along with the tune, thrusts out her chin, takes a deep breath, and smiles, then… nothing.

Nothing can persuade her body to fulfil its duty and perform the steps that she had been dying to complete since… the beginning of time. Alison grunts in frustration as she gazes out into the blackness, and the void stares back. Beyond it there are people, real people. Her mum and dad and little brother George amongst them, and all the other performers' families and members of the dance school. They are all there and they are waiting for her. Waiting for her to start the whole show.

Her mind rests upon Olivia, the girl whose role she had inherited, and she wondered how she was feeling, holed up in bed, her leg encased from toe to hip in plaster.

Alison flushed remembering that she had not been to see her since the accident.

Her mind dragged her back to that day, forced her to dwell on what it had been like to be there. When she had seen the bone sticking out of the flesh, and how her stillness had been pierced by Olivia's screams of agony. She had comforted herself with the fact that she had been able to help by holding her friend's hand until help had arrived.

"Don't leave me, Allie," Olivia had whimpered to her in between screams and tears.

"I won't, I won't; I'm here. Somebody call an ambulance,"

Alison had bellowed, ushering away stampeding footsteps.

Alison had been at pain to make her friend comfortable, creating a makeshift pillow from her own stretched out cardie and pushing it under Olivia's head.

"Am I going to die?" Olivia wanted to know at one point and Alison's mouth had dried up. She forced a shaky smile but words were quite beyond her reach.

Alison watched over her friend, she thought how pale she looked, but still beautiful, she had noticed. It was a thing of wonder that even when the tears and snot had mingled into a rivulet that made its steady way across her cheeks, Olivia managed to look more beautiful than ever before. Words like damsel, distress and princess played on her mind until the tug on Alison's hand increased in force, lockstep with the volume of Olivia's screams until Alison too was gasping for air and crying out in pain.

Everyone that day had surveyed the scene, and blood had been everywhere. All over the stairs and across the stage. After it was over, and Olivia was well on her way to hospital, Alison had thrown away her cardie rather than get it washed, telling her mum that it had been stolen during classes. She didn't want any reminders of that day, thank you very much. She spent the rest of the day wondering how long it might take for a broken leg to mend. It had all been so unfortunate for Olivia, but Alison could not allow that to get in the way of the opportunity it had afforded. Obviously she had jumped at the chance when she had been asked to take her friend's place on stage.

A chair grates across the auditorium floor, and the noise calls Alison back to the present. She looks up. The heat of the stage lights beat down on her shoulders, making her feel uncomfortable and strangely out of place. The glow is yellow, not white as she had always remembered them. They were harsh and made it difficult to see far, her vision ending at the edge of the stage.

"Just as well really. I don't want to see anybody right now, or to know what they're thinking. I'm making such a mess of things," she sighs.

The sound of her own rasping breath fills her ears. Her chest heaves and her heart thumps, as if it finds the promise of life outside of her ribcage more appealing than life within it.

"Come on Allie, you can do this," she thinks, but her body remains in refusal mode. Her feet are almost growing roots, and she imagines them busily burrowing themselves deep into the dark wooden boards of the stage.

Her eyes swivel across the auditorium. The whole room seems to have expanded, or was it that she had diminished in some way?

"I wish I'd never tried out for this bloody part," she says to herself. Her legs tremble so much she thought at one point that she might crumple to the floor. She eyes again the dark wood that make up the stage. As usual, it is covered by an ancient film of dirt that defied cleanliness, no matter how well, or how often it had been swept and mopped and polished.

"OMG, I can't believe I didn't notice that the stage is stained with Olivia's blood, and I'm standing in it." Alison's jaw falls open.

There's no business, like show business...

The pianist pounds on the keys making it obvious that she has played the introduction several times in a row already.

"Why isn't she moving?" anonymous voices make their way on stage from the audience.

Loud whispers join the original ones, assaulting her ear drums with spite.

"You can dress up a pig as much as you want, but it's only

ever gonna be a better relation of the hogs in the woods."

"I just knew they shouldn't have had her in that role."

"What were they thinking? She's no Olivia, is she?"

The words fly across the space and sting her, like the time she had knocked over Grandma's drink, and been slapped hard across the face.

A stifled giggle pierces the darkness and moves like a virus until a chorus of laughter engulfs the entire room.

At one side of the stage, someone wearing a red sequinned top is flapping their arms about. "Alison, you need to start dancing. Just like we practiced."

The voice is harsh and demanding, forced out between clenched teeth. She recognises it immediately - Mrs Robinster. Even from where she stands, Alison can smell the cigarettes and unwashed feet that accompany her every movement.

All the other teachers complain about her when she isn't around.

"Somebody should tell her," they all agreed but no one ever dared to do it.

Alison didn't like the teachers. They had given the principal role to Olivia, as if there had never been any suggestion of it going to anybody else. In four years, they had never even acknowledged her existence, until a few weeks ago when she had taken matters into her own hands. Had created her own opportunities in life by helping Olivia to experience that 'little accident' during rehearsals.

She flushes with shame, lowering her eyes, considering her actions and their impact. "I'm so sorry, Olivia. I didn't mean to... I just needed to get you out of the picture, just for a little while," Alison whispers to herself, blinking back tears.

Amongst the silhouette of the audience, she glimpses Olivia's mother. She alone is seated in a pool of light. A replica of her daughter. She of the blonde hair, blue eyes and long slim legs. A scowl replaces her broad smile, revealing the contour of her perfect white teeth. Something blue appears in her hands and flashes across the room. No one notices but Alison, who feels a sharp pain burst inside her skull and ricochet around her body.

She cries out in shock and grabs the sides of her temple. "Arggh, my head. It feels like my head is going to explode."

But it doesn't. Instead, there's a new sound. It is close by. Lower than a murmur, less than a whisper, but to Alison it resembles an explosion in a warehouse. There it is again. As if a tap has been left on. No, not fully on. That would have sounded more like a gush, a gurgle but this was a slight flow.

It starts at the bottom of her blue leotard, making a dark mark across her gusset and follows the line of her thighs and calves until it forms a large yellow puddle near her brightly polished tap shoes. What was once warm is quickly replaced by wetness and cold.

From the audience comes, an eruption of laughter.

"Bring the curtains down," shouts a female voice backstage.

"Lower them now!" additional voices sounding desperate. Alison didn't recognise any of them in particular, but it was sure to be some of the many teachers who are working that day.

A high-pitched voice bawls out, "I can't shift the curtains they're stuck."

"Get her off! Get her off!" said another teacher, her voice hoarse from fear and accountability.

Heavy steps panic their way towards her and before she is aware Alison feels the cold damp clasp of Mrs. Robinster's clutches dragging her away from the front of the stage.

She looks over her shoulder towards the place of her demise, the bloody stain darker than ever, then beyond the stain into the audience, whilst the sound of laughter echoes around the auditorium.

"Where's the light? Where's Olivia's mum?" Alison calls out. The light that had once settled on Olivia's mum was gone and the area beyond it once more in eternal blackness.

"There's one every damned year," said Mrs Robinster, ignoring Alison's pleas, her nose wrinkling up in disgust. "I know, I know just be grateful for small mercies at least it's only number ones, and not like 2015," her beefy assistant answers. She reaches out her hand to signal for help. "Bucket!"

Made by Nazmin Pirbhai

Bisman (Blue)

by *Sandra Pollock OBE*

The dawn welcomed her with its bright pink glow, accompanied by a fresh cool breeze that snuck under the blanket she had so tightly wrapped around herself the night before.

The gardener could always be relied on to leave a few soft coverings in the shed for them. He had done that ever since they were children and would want to sleep outside during summer nights.

Her groggy mind resisted her call to bring itself to attention, so she could remember exactly why she was out in the woods this morning. But as the memories came back to her in vivid shards, sharp and stabbing, punching their way into her thoughts, she wished she didn't remember.

With each image came a deeper sense of pain, reflection, and embarrassment, ripping their way through her heart and chest, taking away her ability to breathe.

No one had even come out to find her. Not that she would have allowed them to see the glimmering of her being. Ha! She could see them, but they could not see her unless she allowed them to. This would be her revenge, but she would have to get the stone back first.

She had believed them, drawn into their labyrinth of lies. He had no intention of caring for her; he just wanted the gem. The blue stone that kept their worlds in place. Fool! How could she not see through him?

The rugged bark of the coconut tree somehow felt comforting against her skin. Comfort was not what she deserved but she allowed it to reach her. Warm streaks slid down her cheeks. Her body convulsed as her unwilling sobs escaped her tightly closed lips. This was her land, her strength, and she had given it away for a promise. For a lie.

It was midday when she woke again to the calling of Bisman. Crying out across the clouded sky to reach her.

"I hear you. Where are you? I'm coming, show me the way."

The blanket fell, softly crumpling over the grass that covered the warm soil beneath, as the wind lifted her into the sky. A gentle swoosh was all that could be heard, and she was gone. The trees covered her until she was too high for them, then the clouds lowered themselves to protect her from praying eyes. But the whole within her where Bisman belonged could not be hidden.

Kwame sat in the front of the house. Cool water eased down his throat as he took liquid respite from the sun. Its heat seemed more fierce than usual today.

"Where is that worthless pixie?" He knew that she would not be far away. His lips twitched into a sneer. He had finally won. Years of planning and plotting. "It would all be mine by the setting of the sun."

His eyes rested on a large deep, dark stone, sitting in the see-through case at the centre of the wooden table. His eyes focused on it again. *Was this thing growing? I'm sure it was smaller last night.*

A flash of golden light radiated from the stone. The glass case that held it was shattered. The stone was now twice its size.

Chair, table and Kwame himself flew back, toppling over. Wide eyed, he jumped to his feet and looked around. Had someone attacked him? There was no one to be seen.

A penetrating pain ripped through his skull. Toppling feet-over-head, arms stretched out, his fingers reaching, grabbing for anything to steady him, until the sudden cracking thud, as his head and body were stopped as they met the ground. Before he could do anything, he became aware of a huge dark shadow moving above him.

The sound of a voice screaming filled his ears. At first, he could not make out what the voice was saying. The language was strange, old. Then he knew. It was her. She was here. What was she doing?

"No, Bisman, no. Not for give you strength. No! Not for give you peace. No. No, Bisman. Come back to me, Bisman. Forgive. It, foolish. Bisman, forgive. I forgive it, Bisman, No. No...!"

Excruciating pain tore through Kwame. The lower half of his body felt on fire. He almost blacked out, but her relentless screaming seemed to break through his thoughts and keep his mind with him.

Looking down at himself, all he could now see was the dark crystal engulfing his body. Well, it looked like the dark crystal he had ripped from her the night before, when she was in his arms in gentle slumber, having given herself to him so completely. The stone he had envied all his life. The one he had heard would bring him immense power, magic, and eternal control. But now it was growing larger and larger. Literally engulfing his entire body, eating him alive. What had he done wrong?

The crystal shook from side to side and with it the ground shook beneath his body, quaking, rumbling and groaning. Kwame's pain intensified. His screams of agony joined with the wailing of the whole planet as the stone dug itself deeper and deeper into the ground, expanding in size as it did. Even her voice was no longer helping to hold back his consciousness or the pain. And then he knew nothing. But the ground still shook and rumbled.

Malika took to the sky again, this time not pleading but singing and dancing in the hope that Bisman would soon settle its anger.

Malika sang for many days and nights. Years it would have seemed to some, and while she did the land beneath her was changed: cracked, split, upturned, ravaged, and burned. Green turned to ash and sand to glass, as the anger and the pain Bisman felt from being torn from its rightful placed was soothed.

On the day of the 7th moon, when the smoke from the burnt and scorched land hung between the ocean and the sky, in the place where no trees were there to hold her and give her rest, she found Bisman again.

Smaller, clear, shimmering and calm. It rose up to meet her.

Malika stopped mid-motion of her singing and dancing and turned to face Bisman, holding herself open, and waited, arms outstretched.

Bisman charged forward, full velocity, burning away everything in its way. The air itself hissed and smoked in its path.

For a second Malika feared that she would be destroyed in its anger. But she knew she would have to face its wrath if that was to be. She had allowed it to be taken. She had given it away. Given away her power.

But at about two feet, Bisman abruptly stopped in front of her. It began to turn around and around. Flipping over and over as though it was her duty to inspect it for purity. Then Bisman stopped. The light within it became brighter, yet a deeper shade of blue. And there, to the left of centre, she saw it, a brown rugged shape of a man. A flash of light and it was gone.

Malika reached out and took Bisman in her hands. It was small again now, the size of a peach. Malika placed it at the centre of her throat, where it had been positioned from the dawn of time and had stayed for millennia.

The clouds cleared. The rains came and the land began to return to its fruitfulness.

SanRoo Publishing

To find out more about SanRoo Publishing
visit our website at:

www.sanroopublishing.co.uk

Follow us on Facebook @acalltowrite

or on Twitter @SanRooWriters

SanRoo Publishing
is part of
Inspiring You C.I.C.

26 Bramble Way, Leicester, LE3 2GY
Registered Company No. : 1021381

CPSIA information can be obtained
at www.ICGtesting.com
Printed in the USA
BVHW091652030621
608739BV00010B/1883